EAST OF THE SUN
AND WEST OF THE MOON

TO

JAMES SIMPSON

WHO MADE THIS TRIP POSSIBLE. OUR ONE
REGRET IS THAT HE WAS UNABLE TO
BE OUR COMPANION ON IT

CONTENTS

EAST OF THE SUN
AND WEST OF THE MOON

CHAPTER I

PLEASURES OF ANTICIPATION

"Now the girths and ropes are tested,
Now they pack their last supplies."
—RUDYARD KIPLING.

WHEN I was defeated for Governor of New York
I got an involuntary holiday, and fortunately my
brother Kermit could adjust his affairs and free himself for the coming year. For years he and I had been
planning to make an expedition together. Time and
again we had to put it off, because when one could
go, the other could not. This year conditions shaped
themselves to make it possible.

There were many delightful short trips we could
have taken with reasonable comfort. We decided,
however, that these should be saved for a later day
when we had qualified for the grandfather class. We
felt we should take the hard trek now when we were
still in good condition physically, before we "carried
too much weight for age."

Though I have done a certain amount of roughing
it and hunting during my life, compared to Kermit
I am a beginner. Every continent has seen the smoke
of his camp-fires. He was on the expeditions made
by my father to Africa and South America. His
business is shipping, which takes him all over the

1

world, and as a result he has been able in the course of his work to hunt in India, Manchuria, and various parts of the United States and Mexico.

Though hunting in itself is great sport, without the scientific aspect as well it loses much of its charm. Therefore, we decided that any expedition we made would be organized along scientific lines. Both Kermit and I are much interested in natural history and have been for years. Through my father, originally, we met naturalists the world over. When I was knee-high to the proverbial grasshopper I remember delightful days spent with John Burroughs and others, who saw in the woods ten times more than the ordinary individual sees.

Our thoughts turned to central Asia. As a matter of fact, this had always been the Mecca of our desires. Though one of the oldest countries in the world, it is one of the least known. In the northern part the Mongol tribes originated, who swept like flame over Asia and half of Europe. Through it the great caravan routes run, over which trade passed before Rome was founded, when Egypt was the world-power, and elephants were hunted on the Euphrates. These caravan routes are practically the same to-day as they were when a few adventurous Europeans pushed east over them in the late Middle Ages.

Roy Chapman Andrews and his expedition have covered the Gobi desert and the surrounding territory, and will reach the Altai mountains, and probably Dzungaria. It would have been duplication of effort for us to strike for the same country, so we decided we would make our general objective farther south and west.

Besides this we had in our minds Kipling's verse from "The Feet of the Young Men":

"Do you know the world's white rooftree—do you know that
    windy rift
  Where the baffling mountain eddies chop and change?
Do you know the long day's patience, belly-down on frozen
    drift,
  While the head of heads is feeding out of range?
It is there that I am going, where the boulders and snow lie,
  With a trusty, nimble tracker that I know.
I have sworn an oath, to keep it, on the Horns of Ovis Poli,
  For the Red Gods call me out, and I must go."

We therefore fixed on the Pamirs, Turkestan, and the Tian Shan mountains as our objectives. There in the Pamirs lives ovis poli, which is conceded by sportsmen the world over to be one of the finest of all game trophies. Ovis poli is the great wild sheep of Marco Polo, the "father and mother" of all the wild sheep. He represents the elder branch of the family of which our bighorn is a member, and makes our bighorn look, in comparison, a small animal. He lives in the barren, treeless Pamirs. He was originally discovered about 1256 by Marco Polo, hence the name. Marco Polo says:

3

There are great numbers of wild beasts, among others wild sheep of great size, whose horns are good six palms in length. . . . This plain is called Pamier, and you ride across it for twelve days together, finding nothing but desert without habitation or any green thing, so that travellers are obliged to carry with them whatsoever they have need of.

For a long time this was considered a romance, for any one was willing to prove that no such animal could exist. It was allotted a place with the unicorn and the phœnix. At last, some six hundred years later, Lieutenant John Wood, an English officer, made his way into the country, shot a sheep, and proved that Marco Milione—at least in this instance —was speaking the truth. Indeed, if anything, he was understating the case, for whereas he says that "these great sheep have horns six hands in length," the record head, a pick-up, is seventy-five inches. This head belonged to Lord Roberts, the famous "Little Bobs of Kandahar," and was given him by the Emir of Afghanistan. Not only is Marco Polo correct where he describes the wild sheep but also the customs of the natives which he mentions are practically unchanged from that day to this. Poor Polo, like many another who has told the unknown truth, was branded a colossal liar by his generation.

Beyond the Pamirs, the "world's white rooftree," lies the plain of Turkestan. There the barren, sandy waste of the Takla Mahan desert is broken only by the oases and jungles that fringe the streams. These rivers, turbulent, muddy torrents when they leave the mountains, gradually shrink as they wind their way through the plain until they finally disappear in brackish marshes in the desert. In the jungles are Yarkand stag and many small animals and birds. Still farther north, running across northern Turkestan, lie the Tian Shan mountains, where two other great sheep live—the ovis ammon karelini and the ovis ammon littledalei. There also lives the greatest of all the ibex, whose horns measure between fifty and sixty inches. Besides these, in this territory are snow-leopards, the great brown bear, the Siberian roe, the Asiatic wapiti, and many other forms of wild life.

On this trek we would strike all climates, from the bitter weather of snow-swept mountains to the blazing heat of sand-drifted deserts and jungle-covered river-bottoms. The country was exceedingly interesting from a scientific standpoint, because no comprehensive American expedition had ever covered it, and there were to all intents and purposes no collections of the wild life in our museums.

My brother Kermit and I were in no position to finance an undertaking of this sort ourselves. Fortunately for us, the Field Museum of Natural History in Chicago was interested in our plans, and Mr. Stanley Field and Mr. Davies, director of the museum, went to Mr. James Simpson to see if the money could be raised for the undertaking. Mr.

Simpson not only believes very strongly in out-of-door life but also is a great advocate and backer of scientific enterprise. Within an hour he had agreed to furnish the financial support, and the James Simpson-Roosevelts-Field Museum Expedition was born.

One of the real problems that confronted us on the trails of central Asia was the difficulty of transporting equipment and supplies. Every additional white man, of course, greatly increased the baggage that must be carried. For this reason we had to keep our white personnel to a minimum. We decided, therefore, that besides ourselves we would be able to take only two others. Our first choice was George K. Cherrie, a man of marked attainments as a scientist. Cherrie was with my father and Kermit on their South American expedition. We got in touch with him at once, and were delighted when he not only agreed to come but was as enthusiastic as either of us.

For the fourth member, we asked a lifelong friend, Suydam Cutting, who took photography for his particular work. Parenthetically, just before we left the United States, Cutting and his brother won the National Court Tennis Championship, and when he returned he won the singles.

Perhaps one of the most interesting aspects of the expedition, from a scientific standpoint, was the fact that it formed a link in the great study that is now in progress to determine the course of migration of animal life to this continent. In prehistoric times Asia and North America were connected by a land bridge which stretched across the Bering Straits. The theory is that most of our mammal forms, including man, originated on the great central Asian plateau, worked north following the receding icecap, migrated across the land bridge, and then spread south over this continent. In other words, our wapiti is descended from the ancestor of the Asiatic wapiti, and our Indian from far-distant tribesmen of central Asia. What I say does not mean, of course, that our forms are descended from the forms now in existence in Asia, any more than man is descended from any existing species of anthropoid ape. It means that a common ancestor existed from which the present types evolved, and from which in many cases both have varied largely. Naturally, as environs tend to influence variation, those animals which remained in the place in which the original stock lived have, as a rule, varied least. In this country an extensive and comprehensive study of mammal, bird, and reptile life has been made. In Asia, the Roy Chapman Andrews expeditions have collected exhaustively the northern and central varieties. The Field Museum Expedition adds the final link to the chain by collecting the southwestern Asiatic specimens. Our scientists in this country will then have at their disposal for study a more or less complete series, stretching from the table-lands of southwestern Asia north, and then down through our continent. From this, in all probability, they will not only be able to prove their theory but also to work out many other interesting problems concerning variation.

The next problem confronting us was to determine our route and get our passports. Getting into this part of Asia is difficult at best. Three ways lie open. One is across China, one across Russia, and one over the Himalayan passes north of the Vale of Kashmir. To cross China we would have had to travel five months by caravan to reach our hunting-grounds. The transportation of supplies we thought would be chancy through the "Land of the Brown Bear."

We therefore decided to apply for permission to the British Government to cross the mountain wall that protects India on the north. Over these mountains, at one point or another, the majority of the invaders of India have poured since the Aryans who left us the Vedic hymns flooded down in pre-historic times to the Punjab. Here the distances are not so great but "every mile stands on end." Again three choices offered themselves. We could go over the Hunza Pass, or through the Leh-Karakoram route, or endeavor to work our way up through Afghanistan. The first of these, the Hunza route, seemed to us the most desirable for it landed us directly in the poli country, the Tagdum-Bash Pamirs. This, however, proved impossible, for two Dutch mountain-climbers, the Vissers, had already

8

organized an expedition to explore this region, and had obtained permits to use this pass. Because of the great difficulty in transporting supplies, only one expedition was permitted to go through there that year. We then had left open to us the Leh-Karakoram and the Afghanistan routes. The Afghanistan route was very difficult, and the natives uncertain, to put it mildly. We did not wish to be "collected" ourselves before we had a chance to collect any animals, so when we failed of permission to use the Hunza we applied for permits to go by the Leh-Karakoram route.

The Viceroy of India, Lord Reading, and the British Government most kindly gave us permission. This, of course, was only part of the permits we needed, for in the mid-Himalayas the sovereignty changes from British to Chinese, and Turkestan and the Tian Shan are part of the Chinese Republic. For poli-hunting, too, we might have to go to the Russian Pamirs, so Russian passports were necessary.

We went to the Chinese Legation. They immediately extended to us every courtesy. Not only did Minister Sze help us officially but also he put us in touch with personal friends of his who were acquainted with some parts of the country through which we intended to travel.

Mr. Sze told us frankly that he was not sure how much he could do, as Turkestan is a very long way

9

from the seat of government in China, and the reins of authority are but lightly held. He said that he would cable to Pekin. Knowing the effect an impressive document has on people in the back-eddies of the world, we asked him also to draw up for us the most gorgeous "to whom it may concern" he could make. He entered into the plan, and found in the attic of the legation a form of credentials long abandoned but resplendent with gold lettering and seals. On it he wrote a long and flowery description of us. More than once this stood us in good stead, for even when the natives could not read they were awed by its splendor.

As there was no Russian representative in the United States, we had to wait for the Russian visas until we reached England.

Naturally, we were on tenter-hooks while getting our permits, for any slip-up would have driven the expedition on the rocks, and it was impossible for us to wait and undertake it "some other year." As William the Silent observed when he decided to strike for the Crown of England, it was a case of "Aut nunc aut nuncquam." There was general rejoicing in the Roosevelt family when word came that everything was arranged.

At about this time we made the announcement of our plans. There are those who say that Americans have lost the pioneer spirit. I doubt if they would maintain this had they seen the flood of letters that were received by the museum, Simpson, Kermit, Cherrie, and myself. Literally hundreds of people from all over the country wrote asking to go on the expedition. Nearly all of them either volunteered to go without pay or to pay their expenses. Jew and Gentile, lawyer and dock-hand, city-dweller from the East and rancher from Idaho, they "yearned beyond the sky-line where the strange roads go down." Indeed, we even had applications from Canada, France, Russia, and Germany. Here in this country, a large group were young fellows just graduating from college. Next to them in point of numbers came ex-soldiers, excellent men, whom we would have been glad to have with us. Then there were hunting-men, and scientific and outdoor men of all types; one minister applied to go as a missionary. Nor was this entirely confined to the male sex, for a number of women, evidently inspired by the exploits of the women explorers of this century, wrote to us. One, I recall, wished to be a cook. Another felt that stenographic work would be valuable. Some men went so far as to come to New York to apply in person. Many of these people would have done well on the expedition but, in a country where every additional ounce of baggage counts against you, it is necessary to cut personnel to the bone, so we had to refuse all applications.

Besides these came offers and suggestions of every kind and description. They ranged from advice as to books that we should take on the trip to special remedies for problematical ailments. Naturally, a large part of them were taken up with suggestions for rifles and equipment. Perhaps there is no more persistent crank than the rifle crank. He has more theories to the square inch than there are hairs on a dog's back. One of these wrote to say that he had arranged a rifle-trap by which the game could be made to shoot itself.

In addition to those who wished to give us things, there were the usual host who wished us to give them things. Countless letters came in asking us to bring the writer some "souvenir" when we returned. One man wanted a dog, another wanted postage-stamps of the locality. There are dogs in the Pamirs, but I am afraid that the man who was in search of postage-stamps will have to wait many a long year before his ambition is realized.

In selecting our outfit, we took as our first principle that we must keep the bulk and weight down to the lowest extent consistent with attaining the results we desired, and we decided to take from this country only those articles which we felt we might not be able to get in India.

First of all, of course, the question of rifles came up. Originally we intended to take .405 Winchesters, but though the smashing power of this arm is very great, the trajectory is hardly flat enough for long-range shooting. For this reason we left these rifles in Kashmir for use on our return to India. For central Asia we decided upon two .375 Hoffman arms and two sporting model Springfields. Cherrie took also a combination shotgun and rifle—valuable as a collector's gun—and an extra 16-gauge shotgun. For all the various arms we carried a total of some 3,000 rounds of ammunition.

Our bedding-rolls were water-proof envelopes with eider-down between the blankets. They were excellent, and kept us warm even in the bitterest weather. We took telescopes, Zeiss binoculars, three little still cameras, an Akeley movie camera, the regulation army emergency ration, saddles, compasses, and a number of other small articles.

In the high altitudes where air is scant it is very difficult to cook. An onion can be boiled literally for hours and still remains hard as a rock. To cure this we bought a patent pressure cooker. It was excellent. Not only did it give us hot food but it was so simple and strong that even a native could understand it and could not break it.

The scientific equipment consisted mainly of skinning-tools, preservatives for the various specimens, and traps for the smaller animals. For bait for the traps Cherrie took peanut butter and raisins.

For literature we took the proverbial standbys: the Bible, Shakespeare, and "Pilgrim's Progress," flanked by an odd assortment of works: "The Ingoldsby Legends," "Plutarch's Lives," "Mr. Midshipman Easy," "The Cloister and the Hearth," Robinson's poetry, Kipling's poetry, some of Molière's comedies, and a number of others selected equally at random. They were cloth-covered editions, easy to carry, and valuable only for their contents.

An interesting feature of our equipment were four cougar hounds. Kermit had suggested that it might be a good plan to take hounds, and try to hunt the varmints of central Asia with them. There is in central Asia a very rare tiger which no white man has ever shot. Travellers have occasionally seen its tracks. We thought if we were fortunate enough to come on signs of this animal, we might get it with hounds when we would stand no chance with other methods.

We bought, therefore, two hounds from an old hunter in Montana, Bob Bakker. Two more dogs were given us by Tom McHenry, of Mississippi. The latter were descendants of the famous Rainey pack that was used in Africa.

We had many amusing times with the dogs. To begin with, my brother lives in New York City and I live in the country. Therefore, it was foreordained through the ages that when they came East they should stay with me until the time came for them to go. My wife runs the place in the country. On it she has, besides four children, two dogs of which she is very fond. Early in the proceedings, she ad-

vised us that the hounds were not to be kept at
Oyster Bay. We felt that it was wiser not to debate
the matter, so we said nothing. Fortunately, they
arrived the day I was going to Chicago, so I merely
let her know the dogs had come and then left town.
I think the best account of what happened then is
given in the following letter from my wife to my
sister, Mrs. Longworth:

DEAR SISTER,

So far, I haven't had much to do helping in the arrangements for the trip, but what a change to-day! When they first
planned to hunt the long-haired tiger with cougar hounds, I
said it was a grand idea, provided I did not have to take care
of any stray hounds out here. Ted and Kermit didn't say much
in direct reply, but talked a great deal about the rarity and
phenomenal value of the Montana hounds—equalled only by
those of Mississippi.

Time went on. Day before yesterday, Ted said: "Oh, by
the way, the hounds are coming to-morrow. You can arrange
about them all right, of course!" I said feebly: "How many?"
Ted said: "Maybe a couple from Montana, maybe a couple
from Mississippi. Four perhaps—yes, that's it, four—nice
dogs, very." Then he took the train for Chicago.

Well, the hounds spent the night in Kermit's laundry in
town, and Dick [Doctor Derby] was persuaded to take them
out to me in his car with Summers [Kermit's chauffeur].

When they got here, I heard a racket such as never was,
and went out to find our entire household gathered to admire
two of the most delightful bloodhoundish animals I ever saw.
My two puppies were watching most disapprovingly from the
top of a hill, and later they retired discreetly to their kennels.

Summers said to me: "The other two dogs will be here to-
morrow, madam. Of course you won't want to change their

diet. They are accustomed to seven pounds of meat apiece daily. Horse-flesh. If you try to have it cooked in the house you won't be able to remain indoors. It is rather strong, but excellent for the hounds. They should be taken for a run every day for exercise, but you mustn't do it, madam—you couldn't hold them."

I spent that afternoon motoring all around in a vain search for the huntsman of the —— Kennels, whom I hoped to be able to persuade to help me out with the food. Finally, I got him on the telephone, and sounded exactly like Aunt —— buying tickets for Cuba.

"My husband is going hunting in central Asia . . . a most interesting experiment . . . cougar hounds, after long-haired tiger. . . . The hounds are here now. . . . My husband has gone to Chicago. . . . I know nothing. . . . Of course *you* know more about hounds than any one. . . . Oh! if you only *would*. . . ."

He was coming around next morning at eight-thirty to see those hounds. I had had two strenuous days in town, and had been looking forward to oversleeping next morning, but, needless to say, I was down-stairs waiting, hoping that I could arrange to get, for this week and next, twenty-eight pounds a day of cooked horse.

The telephone rang. He was detained, but would be over in the afternoon. I had been going out that afternoon, but what did that matter? I stayed in, and he never came at all. Those dogs ate beef and dog-biscuit, and were glad to get it. They didn't get seven pounds apiece a day either!

In addition to all this, and more besides, the children are having their Easter vacation.

One reason I want to come to see you is the idea of the long peaceful train journey between New York and Washington!

E.

My wife put these dogs in the barn. She put the two strongest in the strongest shed she had. The next morning they had broken down most of the shed, and were almost loose. She then had them chained with heavy iron chains. One of them broke his chain. She then had them chained together, on the theory that if they got away, they would not run so far. This was almost disastrous, because they thereupon proceeded to try to eat each other up!

The cheapest way to get our equipment, including the hounds, to India was to send it direct over one of my brother's lines to Karachi. Cherrie agreed to go with it. The last two days before Cherrie's departure we spent in feverish packing. We checked everything once, then checked it back again. We kept lists of every box. Eventually, Cutting was detailed to paint numbers on our boxes. He did it thoroughly—so thoroughly, in fact, that he partially painted one child and a library chair as well.

On the morning of the day that Cherrie's boat went, we all gathered at Kermit's house, where the equipment had been assembled. We shoved the last things into a trunk and then, in three automobiles, went down to see Cherrie off. We divided the cougar hounds between the automobiles. One sat on my lap in the front seat of our car. When we got to the pier we found that there was only an iron gangway, which the dogs could not climb, so we struggled on board, each with a cougar hound over his shoulder. We took them forward and left them tied to stanchions.

17

Next Saturday, April 11, Kermit, Suydam Cutting, and I sailed on the *Leviathan*.

When we reached England, the first and most important thing we had to do was to get our passports to the Russian Pamirs, where we believed the largest ovis poli would be found. We went at once to the headquarters of the Russian Trade Delegation, where Mr. Rakovsky, the envoy, was very cordial. We presented our letters, and he told us that he would be glad to give us the permit. We stayed to tea with him. Before the revolution he had been head of a big mill in Russia, and he discussed economic conditions the world over with wide knowledge. What struck me most about the offices of the delegation was the number of portraits, busts, and photographs of Lenin that were everywhere. As far as this delegation is concerned, Lenin stands first, and there are no seconds.

We then called on various hunters, travellers, and naturalists. It was delightful meeting them, and they were invariably kind and helpful. They put themselves out to aid us in every way. They recommended for our party natives whom they knew, advised on the best passes and trails, and suggested equipment. As they talked you could see they imagined themselves back, pushing through snow-covered mountain passes, and tramping in dust clouds over sere, sun-dried plains.

We stopped in Paris just long enough to buy a few

odds and ends. These consisted mainly of presents for the natives. Some of the country where we intended to hunt is so far from civilization that money means little to the tribes who live there. We purchased an assortment of knives, cheap watches, and similar articles. The best of these were the most gorgeous buttons that ever graced a gown. They were every color of the rainbow. There was not a subdued note amongst the lot. The colors were chosen not to blend but to clash.

From Paris we went to Marseilles, where we took ship for the last leg of the trip to India. Travel was light and we had the ship nearly to ourselves. This gave us a splendid chance to study Hindustanee. We had it for breakfast, we had it for lunch, and we had it for dinner. I am not particularly good at languages, and I soon felt as if my mind were like one of those kaleidoscopes in which colored glass is continually shifting into patterns of meaningless design.

The weather was clear, the Mediterranean was sapphire blue. We passed Stromboli at night. It was "acting up," and every few seconds a tongue of red flames stabbed the black of the sky. The birds were migrating north from their winter in Africa, and, though we were out of sight of land, many flew by the ship. One in particular, a dove, came in under the awning and lit on a stanchion. Early one morning I looked out of the port-hole and there, lying to the north, was a rugged coast-line capped with a snow-crowned mountain. It was Crete, the home of the sea-kings, and of one of the oldest civilizations of which we have record.

We passed Port Said, where the real East begins, and where an ethnologist would tear his hair in despair, for every race has blended there for years, with a strange and weird result. Down the Red Sea we cruised, with barren, sun-scorched desert shivering in the heat haze on either hand.

One evening we reached Aden, built in the crater of an extinct volcano. I can imagine no hotter place, for the sun beats down on it and the rock walls guard it from every breeze. In fact, I should think the inhabitants would be inclined to disagree with Kipling when he says:

> "Old Aden, like a barrack stove
> That no one's lit for years and years."

The origin of the town is lost in the shadows of time. It has always been a point of contact between Africa and Asia. People have lived there so long that the valley is one great graveyard, and one cannot dig anywhere without turning up bones. We saw the water-tanks that supplied the old town. They are built of cement, the process for making which is lost, and which is better than any we make to-day. Their origin, like that of the town, is unknown. Behind Aden, up the peninsula, lies Arabia Felix where the Queen of Sheba is supposed to have had her capital.

WEST OF THE MOON

From Aden we cruised over a changeless sea, until early one morning Bombay with its clustered shipping loomed up out of the haze.

The first stage of our Odyssey was finished.

CHAPTER II

FROM THE VALE OF KASHMIR TO THE BARRENS OF LADAKH

THOSE who know India only during the winter months, the tourist season, can form little conception of what the country is like during the summer. In the greater centres of population the old hand-pulled punka has given way to the electric punka, or the simple electric fan. At the stations along the railway, however, you still see the patient punka-coolie squatting outside the station-master's room, tugging at the punka-rope with monotonous regularity, and it is he that to me typifies the great heat of the Indian plains.

When we landed in Bombay this time, on May 11, there was fortunately nothing to oblige us to linger long in the heat, and so, after some strenuous bustling about, making a few final preparations, we pulled out of Cocaba Station at half past four in the afternoon of the very day on which we had arrived. The most valuable acquisition which we made there was the information with which Mr. S. H. Prater, the head of the Bombay Natural History Museum, supplied us. He not only possessed a fund of helpful hints and data but was very ready to impart them to us, a combination not always found.

The captain of the *Homestead*, the freighter on which Cherrie had come over, was waiting for us on the pier at Bombay, and reported that Cherrie and all the equipment had been safely landed at Karachi. We were greatly relieved to hear this, and also to learn the four cougar hounds had gone ashore in better shape than they had come aboard. We were still a little anxious, however, about the manner in which they would weather the train journey across the Sind desert.

Forty-eight hours after leaving Bombay we rolled into Rawal Pindi, and on the 14th of May left there by motor for Srinagar. In winter the cantonments are crowded, but during the hot weather headquarters moves to Murree, a hill station some forty miles distant, where the altitude is 7,000 feet. There we spent a night. The descent thence to the Jhelum River is very precipitous, with a multitude of hair-pin turns, and we were glad indeed to have our friend Barr driving. He had been an aviator during the war, and was one of those fast drivers who yet give you full confidence.

The hillsides were glorious with the pink mountain-oleander, and as we neared the river we came upon masses of purple irises. The Jhelum is here a rushing, turbulent river, much used for driving great logs from Kashmir down to the plains of India. Along its banks grow pomegranates, now in full bloom. The road was everywhere in excellent repair. We

23

passed the customs, and a few hours later entered the famous Vale of Kashmir, and sped along the avenues of poplar-trees that remind one of roads in Lombardy. On either side stretched paddy-fields, some already a bright green. Occasionally we came upon a grove of spreading chenar-trees. The chenar has a leaf like the maple, but grows to great size, and in shape reminds one of an old oak. In the fall the leaves turn vivid red and yellow, as do our maples.

Srinagar is often given that very hackneyed title "The Venice of the East." Any town which has a few canals or a couple of rivers winding through it seems to take particular pride in naming itself the Venice of that particular portion of the globe in which it is situated. Srinagar has numerous canals, on one of which is the Maharajah's palace, a long, ramshackle, rather gingerbready building or series of buildings. Along another are strung the European shops and agencies, and gigantic chenar-trees shade the footpath separating the buildings from the canal.

In London we met Major Blacker, whose book, "Secret Patrol in High Asia," I had read with much interest. Blacker is an officer of the Guides, the famous corps formed by Lumsden, which has won fame and name in all the frontier wars, and afterward added to both in the World War. During the months of his strenuous "secret patrol" he had with him two particularly excellent men, Ahmad Shah and Feroze. The former was squadron sergeant-major, and the latter a corporal. If Ahmad Shah had not been absent so much on detached service, he would undoubtedly have become a native officer. Blacker, besides giving us any amount of valuable advice, also cabled the Guides to get in touch with these two men, both of whom had retired from the army, and arrange for them to accompany us.

They were at the station at Rawal Pindi and, coming up, saluted and reported for duty. Ahmad Shah was tall, erect, and bearded, a soldierly figure in his white turban. Feroze was small and wiry, with "thruster" written all over him, a man who could be counted on to push forward in the face of any obstacle. That night, in talking over plans, they told us they knew of a syce, or groom, in the Guides who they were sure could take charge of the dogs. We straightway wired Colonel Campbell, and next day Fezildin arrived by train from Mardan.

Thus, with Rahima and his brother Khalil, native hunters whom I had secured through Douglas Burden, the important members in our party were assembled. These last two had been Burden's shikaries during a most successful hunting trip which he made a few years ago. He cabled them from New York and they were awaiting us in Srinagar. Tall and lean, they were the very type of the ideal shikary. According to local custom, the shikaries had brought with them from their own village of Bandipur our cook and three permanent coolies to do all the odd jobs around camp, carry the tiffin-basket and thermos bottles on the marches, and make themselves generally useful.

I already knew a little Hindustanee, and Ted and Cutting worked like beavers on the language during the sea-passage. None of our men spoke English, so we were immediately called on to put it into practice. During our first interviews, an officer whom I had known in Mesopotamia, Captain Pim, not only acted as interpreter but had many a useful sidelight to give.

Having laid out for ourselves on this trip an extensive schedule, and being obliged to forego the direct route by Gilgit to the Hunza, it was imperative for us to economize time in every way. It is not possible for an ornithologist to work satisfactorily when he is called upon to be continually on the move. We made our plans, therefore, to march together to Leh and thence over the Karakoram Pass. Once over, Ted and I, travelling light, would hurry across the plains of Turkestan to the Tian Shan mountains, while Cherrie and Cutting would follow along more slowly, stopping a few days wherever they wished to collect. By the time they joined us in the Tekkes Valley, we hoped to have got well started on the groups of ibex, wapiti, mountain-sheep, and Siberian roe deer with which we relied upon providing the museum from the Tian Shan country. It was arranged for Ahmad Shah and Feroze to take charge of the main and slow-moving caravan, while Rahima and Khalil undertook with us the expedition after big game.

In Srinagar Sir John and Lady Wood most hospitably invited us to stay at the Residency, and no one could possibly have been more kind. Both Mr. Avery and Captain Sevenoaks, of Cockburn's Agency, worked like Trojans to hurry us through our preparations. Thus aided, and with Sir John's help in everything, we were enabled to start off for Leh four days after we had reached Kashmir.

In Kashmir most of the transport is by pack-pony, tough, wiry little beasts that carry an average load of 150 pounds over most difficult country. When the passes are in bad shape, you cannot negotiate them with ponies, but must rely on porters. Yakdans, which are wooden boxes covered with cowhide, are the most convenient containers for supplies and personal outfit. The kilta, or round basket, is much lighter, but will not stand rough usage.

It is near Ganderbal—the first stage on the road to Leh—that the possibility of motor transport ends. We sent our equipment there by boat on May 18, and followed by automobile some hours later. Early next morning we loaded our food and our scientific equipment onto sixty ponies, and set off up the Sind Valley. The dogs were wild with joy at being once more at large; they had been over two months en route from their homes in Montana and Mississippi. They jumped into the irrigation ditches, and raced up hills, coming back now and again to wag their tails at us.

It would be difficult to imagine more ideal conditions for starting off on a hunting trip. The Sind Valley is narrow and fertile; on the south side the mountains are tree-covered, on the north they are barren; the crests are white with snow. The river boils down between stony banks, now narrow and turbulent, now humming over shallows. There is much cultivation, little stone-enclosed fields of rice or wheat, but the glory of the valley is its trees. Centuries old they must be, chenar and willow. We generally camped beneath some grove of patriarchs, which might well have cast their shade upon Lalla Rookh.

There was a great deal of bird life, and Cherrie was kept busy, for we wished to send back from Leh something that would prove to the Field Museum that we had not delayed in starting to work. Indeed, Cherrie had already returned a first consignment consisting of four different species of hawk which he had shot in the Red Sea from the decks of the *Homestead.*

The sombre raven accompanied us everywhere, and there were many gaily clothed strangers. There were several old friends, too, among the birds, chief

37415

of which was the little water-wagtail, whose intimate acquaintance I first made in central Africa, sixteen years ago. He is such a cheerful, friendly fellow that it is not pleasant to contemplate "collecting" him. He will hop about and wag his tail within a few feet of you in a most confiding manner. Ted and I spent much time watching a couple of water-ouzels diving into the stream. It was amazing to see such a small bird dive off a rock into the rushing water and as much as two minutes after come swimming unconcernedly back.

There were plenty of trout in the river, but we had neglected to provide ourselves with a fishing permit, so Ted, the fisherman of the expedition, had to wait until we should have passed out of the region of restricted waters. We didn't do much in the cause of cleanliness because the water was too cold for more than a hurried dip, preceded by a hasty soaping, while precariously balanced on a slippery rock.

We met with but few butterflies, and none of them were gaudy. Dwarf purple irises grew in clusters on the hills and in the fields; wild roses, both pink and white, were abundant, and an occasional field of mustard in bloom wove in its pattern of cloth of gold.

At Baltal, while awaiting favorable conditions to cross the Zoji Pass, we were serenaded with avalanches. First there would be a booming roar, reminiscent of a battery of heavies on the French

front, then, if the avalanche were in sight, you would
see great masses of snow hurtling down the precipices. After a short intermission another salvo of
sound and more plunging snow—two or three such
outbursts would occur in diminishing violence, and
then all would be quiet.

The Zoji La is the most used pass in the great range
of the western Himalayas. It is the low point in a
line of mighty mountains averaging 17,000 feet in altitude, and containing among other peaks the famous
Nanga Parbat, which is 26,620 feet in height. The
winds naturally concentrate on this gap, and the pass
is at times very treacherous. Sudden blizzards sweep
down, and many human lives, and the lives of countless baggage-animals, have paid toll to the Spirits of
the Pass. In winter it is always hazardous, but it
is in March and April that it is most dangerous with
sudden avalanches and unexpected hurricanes. In
the summer months, beginning with June, there is
rarely any cause for anxiety.

Fortunately, after one day's detention, weather
favored us, and we set off as early as we could gather
the ponies which were scattered about the hillside
in search of pasture. Our train was diminished by
the loss of a pony who died from eating poisonous
grass; not an uncommon occurrence, and one much
dreaded by the pony men. The long winding trail
up the pass gave little trouble, save in a few places
where small avalanches had come down across the

track. One such spot seemed at first sight calculated to afford much difficulty, but the little spindle-legged ponies negotiated it with great skill. One turned a complete somersault, doubling his neck beneath him in such a way that it seemed it must be dislocated. Luckily he was brought up by the heavy drifts before he could roll far, and when we dragged him clear, we found he was unhurt. The descent on the farther side of the pass is gradual, and would have been a simple affair but for the deep snow, now rapidly softening under the burning rays of the sun. The ponies were continually plunging a foot through the bedded snow of the trail, and sinking belly-deep. It must have been most exhausting; we bipeds certainly found it so, but the hardy little beasts gave no signs of failing. They wound down the valley, crossing and recrossing the river, which in most places was hidden deep beneath the snow. At such times we would pass over snow bridges, and more than one of these was ominously fissured and threatened to give way, plunging horse and load into the rushing stream below. We all wore snow-glasses, a very necessary precaution. One of the coolies to whom we could supply none came to us next morning with his eyes in bad shape, and several others had suffered to a less degree.

The dogs alone thoroughly enjoyed themselves, for the surface of the snow was sufficiently strong to

bear their weight. We had been a little worried as
to how much the altitude would bother them, but
we might have spared ourselves the anxiety. They
toiled up and down the mountainside, and along the
most hairbreadth ledges, skirting the caravan, and
always choosing to pass on the outside, although the
ponies themselves preferred to keep so near the edge
that not an inch was left of leeway.

We camped on a boulder-strewn hillside, on which
no snow remained. The ponies came in struggling
manfully through the last drifts. Once over on solid
ground we looked to find them well tuckered out.
Not at all; even before their loads were off they
started grazing, although one would have needed a
microscope to determine what fodder they found.

The contrast between the country out of which
we had passed and that in which we now found
ourselves could scarcely have been greater. No
longer were the mountains covered with forests of
pine, nor was the riverside deep in the shade of willow and chenar. On either hand rose barren mountains; the only relief to their monotony was the
snow that covered their crests and lay in the deeper
folds. Riding down these valleys through the abomi-
nation of desolation, one thought of Isaiah, and felt
the true strength of the Bible's old simile of comfort:
"As rivers of water in a dry place, as the shadow of a
great rock in a weary land."

The Ladakhis are adepts in the art of building

32

irrigation canals. Without these canals there would be no human life. They capture the water coming down in the occasional torrents from the mountain-side and lead it off to moisten the little patches of land, which they have freed from stones. Ploughing is a laborious affair; the familiar crooked wooden plough of Biblical times is pulled by horse or steer or yak, or sometimes by a mixed team. The bits of cultivation are of odd shapes: crescent, elliptical, or round. Often this is accounted for in the avoiding of some large rock or hillock, but at other times the shape seems due to a caprice of the ploughman. There were usually poplar-trees bordering the ditches and perhaps a few fruit-trees mingled with them. These green oases were few and far between, and often not more than a couple of acres in extent. On rounding some bend after a particularly long and arid stretch, the sight of this vivid green brought to mind the words of the old Irish song: "Sure a little bit of heaven fell from out the sky one day." The sun was scorching; never have I felt it stronger, but once in the shade the relief was instantaneous, and in a few minutes you were almost chilly.

Bird life was scarcer here. The ravens were still with us, and occasionally we would see a hawk soaring far above. Once it was a great lammergeyer with a spread of eight or nine feet. The wagtail we still found along the streams, and at the oases there were blue pigeons and purple finches. A sparrow closely

33

resembling our English sparrow was the commonest and most abundant of the birds. They often nested in the holes in the cliffs. Ted succeeded in stalking a hawk and adding it to the collection. This was a particularly difficult feat, because we had only shells for the little auxiliary barrel that was fitted into the 16-gauge shotgun for the purpose of collecting small birds. We were in ibex country now and Rahima Loon explained that he had shot them here, but that the heads were small. In any event we had no time for halts, and had resolved to put off ibex-hunting until we should reach the Tian Shan, where the finest heads are to be found. The larger game seen so far consisted of one small black bear, which Ahmed Shah had observed far up on the mountainside when bringing the baggage-train into Baltal. The dogs were still too soft to risk them on a hunt, even if the bear had been full-grown.

We had now passed out of the land of Moham-medanism into that of Buddhism. In Kashmir, although the rulers are Hindus, the great bulk of the population is Moslem, while in Ladakh, almost without exception, they are Buddhists. On the hill above the little collection of mud huts called by courtesy a town clustered the buildings of the monastery. We came across no town without its monastery. We were in the land of the red lama, and sturdy though grimy members of the sect came down to watch with interest our actions, whether we were eating or reading or preparing bird-skins. In these monasteries there are lamas that correspond to the lay brothers of the Roman Catholic orders; they till the fields and collect the rents, while the balance of the lamas spend their time presumably in meditation and prayer.

The most picturesque of these monastic towns is Lamayuru. On top of the hill rise the sacred buildings, flags flying from the roofs; tier upon tier of house and cavern dwellings stretch down from the mountains to the plain. Seen from a distance Lamayuru is most impressive; in the right light there is a touch of Mont Saint Michel about it; but like most sights in the Orient, it is distance that lends an enchantment which is apt to crumble on closer approach.

At Kargil we lost a companion caravan that had been with us since Baltal. The head of it was a hill Rajah of Baltistan; a very pleasant man of about thirty-five or forty. His wife was purdah—veiled—and travelled in a litter completely hidden behind white curtains. Four sturdy hillmen bore the litter, and it was amazing to see them swing along up the Zoji Pass. For her own peace of mind, I hope the lady never looked out to see how close her litter skirted the edge of nothing. A sturdy Mongol-featured nurse trudged or rode behind. The Rajah's two sons and his three-year-old daughter also accompanied him. The boys were splendid-looking young fellows; they rode with the father, while the little girl had a number of different modes of conveyance. Sometimes we saw her riding pickaback on the shoulders of a fine fiercely mustached retainer of her father's. A small wretched-looking monkey also formed part of the train. The Rajah's pipe-bearer was always at hand at a halt, and hastened forward with the long silver hookah packed ready to light. We separated regretfully when the Rajah turned off to his rocky fastness in Baltistan.

There is great attraction in barren mountains and sterile, rock-strewn valleys. It was spring, and yellow crocuses undauntedly showed their heads among the rocks. The Ladakhis we passed had usually a bunch of flowers stuck in cap or hair. Occasionally, there would be a wild-rose bush in bloom; and on the edges of the fields were patches of iris. In the most arid of the valleys there were always times when the air was redolent with the sweet, pungent odor of the artemisia.

Our pack-train had decreased by ten ponies, for we now had only fifty. Sometimes a donkey or a yak would be drafted in. We changed animals every night. The ponies were sturdier and shaggier than those we had had in Kashmir, but I doubt if they were any tougher. We were in the country of pig-tails, and the men in charge of the ponies wore them. They were a cheerful lot, very Mongol in feature, and not at all cleanly. On the back of each man's tunic was a greasy cone-shaped black mark made by his pigtail as it swung to and fro pendulum-wise.

One day we had a woman among our pony-drivers. This is the land of woman's emancipation. No longer was the adult feminine population kept in the background. Women working in the fields straightened up and greeted us as we passed, and once I saw a man and woman laughing and jostling each other as if they were good friends and comrades—something unimaginable in India or Kashmir. The Mohammedan greeting of "Salaam" had given way to "Joolay," to which your response is "Joo."

The custom of polyandry is largely, if not entirely, responsible for the amelioration of woman's lot. Unattractive and distasteful as it may seem to an Occidental mind, there is here a great deal to be said for it. The very fact that it keeps down the population is of primary importance in a land where the number of people that can be supported has a very definite limit. A woman usually has three husbands, although I heard of one instance where there were seven. They are generally brothers. The first husband stands head of the household. Upon his death the wife, if she so desires, can very simply rid herself of the others by divorce.

There must be a great deal of nutrition in the diminutive and all but invisible clumps of grass scattered through the rocks, for the flocks and herds seem well nourished, and the mutton we bought was

37

excellent. The sheep and goats were very small, many adults no larger than a fox-terrier. They were all friendly, and one little black ram adopted us, trotting along perfectly cheerfully among the dogs. We had great difficulty in persuading him to turn back. We noticed a most curious variation in the shape of the horns. In one herd there would be animals with scimitar-shaped horns resembling ibex, another with spiral horns like markhor, and a third with his horns formed like those of mountain-sheep. It would seem as if these characteristics must point to a descent from the wild game of the mountains.

We went off after sharpu a number of times. These animals are about the size of our Rocky Mountain bighorn, but carry no such fine trophy. Their horns branch out sideways and back in a semicircle. A good head will measure between twenty-five and thirty inches long. They often go in large troops. They prefer a slide-rock country, and walking is both difficult and fatiguing along the shale-covered hillsides. The shikaries rather look down upon sharpu-shooting as a sport that requires but little skill, and Rahima Loon said that when hunting them he paid no attention to wind. We saw at least thirty females one afternoon, and a few rams, but the largest had only a twenty-inch horn, and so was not worth collecting.

At Nurla we were most unexpectedly the witnesses of a protracted Buddhist service. One of our men announced that there was going to be a tamasha, or celebration, and we saw a red lama approaching, followed by a nondescript acolyte bearing a shrine. This shrine was placed beneath a tree on a low platform. Above it was hung a Chinese kakemono of Buddhist saints. Several images were placed in front, together with ceremonial platters and daggers and incense-burners. Next a stone altar was constructed—two smaller rocks supporting a long heavy one that was borne onto the scene by several coolies. The head priest opened the ceremony with some droned invocations, and then the first devil appeared; he wore a grotesque mask and capered about every which way, badgering the priest. The entire population of the village had by now gathered, and were seated in a semicircle—the women and children at one end and the men at the other. There seemed to be but little intermingling, although one old patriarchal couple sat together, sharing their enjoyment of the devil's antics. Many of the women had chubby babies on their arms, or in baskets on their backs, and more than one fat pappoose was diligently sucking its thumb.

The head lama and the devil carried on a most complicated warfare, in which the honors seemed remarkably evenly divided. The spectators were vastly amused, laughing when the devil made sudden sallies into their ranks. At length he was subdued and exorcised. The head priest's labors were by no means over, though, for a second lama immediately appeared. His face was whitened with chalk and he was draped in a sheepskin poshteen with the wool outside. Into the circle he pranced amid much laughter, and once more the chief lama entered into conflict. This battle was longer drawn-out and there were numerous skirmishes with the bystanders, greatly to every one's delight. At length this second devil was overcome also, and prostrated as a penitent before the altar. So far everything had been conducted in light vein. It is said that these devil dances are intended educationally. When, a Buddhist dies he has a straight and narrow path to follow. From this path the devils, with their hideous features, attempt to frighten him, but the lamas thus prepare and forewarn him in life that he may not be affrighted and driven aside.

The serious portion of the services now commenced; there was no longer any laughter, but from this time the onlookers joined in chanting the great prayer of the Buddhist faith: "Om mani padme Om"—"The Jewel in the Lotus." The priest went through his mystic signs. He scattered incense, and genuflected before the altar. He then took a small dagger, which he ran through a hole in his cheek, plunging it in up to the hilt, so that the blade appeared between his teeth. Next he took two sabres, and, intoning a dirge-like chant, swung the swords about his head in the approved Cossack style. Suddenly he stripped himself to the waist, placed the point of each sword in the pit of his stomach, and, running a short distance, plunged forward to the ground, balancing himself on the swords. He must have cleverly taken the weight off the points of the sabres through his grasp upon the hilts, for otherwise they would have pierced his intestines. He now appeared much wrought up, and placing the point of one of the swords in his mouth, in such a way that it brought up against his cheek and bulged it out, he flung himself down, apparently supporting himself solely by the sword-point which was distending his cheek. Before he could repeat this performance the two assistant lamas rushed up and took the swords from him.

One of the reformed devils now lay on the ground on his back, with his sheepskin poshteen folded upon his stomach. On top of this poshteen two men placed the altar-stone. The chief priest seized one of the rocks which had supported the altar and dashed this rock down with all his force upon the altar-stone, smashing the altar-stone in two. There was no flaw in the stone, and it weighed a good hundred and fifty pounds, but the devil beneath sprang up none the worse for wear. I imagine the credit must be supposed to lie in the devil's conversion.

The services were closed with further prayers and some dancing to the accompaniment of a three-stringed zither. By now it was almost dark, and the

41

chanting, swaying figures seemed exotic and outlandish as they wound among the apricot-trees with
the white-topped mountains in the background.

The Ladakhi is evidently a great believer in
the efficacy of prayer, but being of a frugal mind,
he wishes to economize effort wherever possible.
Hence, prayer-wheels. By writing a number of
orthodox prayers and enclosing them in a cylinder,
it is possible to so arrange the cylinder that it revolves around a simple axis with a minimum of effort. Each time a prayer revolves it is the same as
if it were verbally repeated. Many of those watching this Buddhist ceremony had prayer-wheels in
their hands. The pony men are often engaged in
spinning yarn all through the day's march, but next
to the distaff it is the most usual thing to see men
busy turning prayer-wheels. They are sometimes set
upon walls, so that any passer-by may achieve merit
by giving them a turn. There are also long walls
built up eight feet high, on whose tops are strewn
prayer-stones. The lamas inscribe the prayers on
these stones, and if the traveller but keeps the wall
on his right hand, all the prayers thereon automati-
cally say themselves for his benefit. These walls are
called manis and appear in the most unexpected
places. They are sometimes as much as three-quarters of a mile in length. The chortens, or dilapidated
mud-and-stone monuments generally seen near the
manis, are burial vaults or tombs. A rich man occu-

pies one to himself. After his body has been burned the lamas take some of the ashes and mould them with clay into the rough likeness of a man. This is placed in the middle of the chorten. With the poor many such effigies are laid in a single chorten.

We had regarded the stretch from Srinagar to Leh as the first leg of the rather centipedal expedition. At Leh, the capital of Ladak, we were to launch off across the mighty main ranges, so the green oasis that marked the town from a distance loomed up very important to us when we approached it on the morning of June 2, just two weeks out from Srinagar. Riding up through the bazaar to the Travellers' Bungalow, we set to work immediately laying out the lines for the bundobust that would take us into Turkestan.

CHAPTER III

OVER THE LOFTY PASSES OF THE HIMALAYAS TO YARKAND

"March by march I puzzled through 'em, turning flanks and
    dodging shoulders,
Hurried on in hope of water, headed back for lack of grass."
—RUDYARD KIPLING.

LEH, where we were to make the final "bundo-
bust" for our climb over the Himalayas, is a little
village of two or three thousand people. As our caravan approached over a sandy plain, the clustered
foliage almost concealed the town. On every side
brown barren foot-hills stretch away, and the lofty
snow-crowned mountains, rampart-like, surround all.
Leh in the summer months is a busy place, and its
population swells to five or six thousand. It is then
that "the snow-bound trade of the north comes
down" through the high passes. Caravans from
Yarkand, Khotan, and Lhassa wind in, to barter
with those that come north from India through the
Zoji Pass. Then the Leh bazaar is a seething throng
of the races of central Asia, and the gossip of the
hinterlands is exchanged as the hookah passes from
hand to hand.

Our entrance into Leh was a problem, not to us,

but to our shikarees. The evening before we reached the town, they came to us and politely suggested that, in accordance with our dignity, we should get out our "store clothes" from the yakdans and enter in style. We explained to them that all we had with us were the dinner-coats and opera-hats we had brought for the benefit of the Ambans and Begs of Turkestan, and that as missionaries lived in Leh and other English people came there quite often, these clothes would not do for eleven o'clock in the morning. To this they reluctantly agreed, but said something must be done. Of course we would not shave, as our beards were being grown for utility, not ornament. However, we did rummage around in our yakdans and take out what we could find. Kermit put on a very heavy pair of knickerbockers and a black four-in-hand cravat. Cutting and Cherrie each wore an equally heavy pair of long trousers intended for autumn in the Tian Shan, and I borrowed an exceedingly large pair of long trousers with a hole in one knee from Cherrie, and set off my brown canvas shirt with a black evening bow cravat. So clad, we rode majestically into Leh. The best that could be said for us is what was said of the native girl in the "Bab Ballads":

> "And tho' the clothes he made her don
> Sat awkwardly a maid upon,
> They were a great improvement on
> The ones he found her in."

45

In Leh the three officials with whom we had to deal were the Tesildar, representing the Kashmir Government, the Bahadur Khan, representing the Indian Government, and the Aksakal, under whom is the traffic north. Of these the last was by far the most interesting. His title, Aksakal, is Turki and means "white-bearded one." His name was Abdullah Shah. He was a lean, brown, fine-featured fellow. His family is Mohammedan. It has been the great family in Leh for generations. Though Mohammedans, they hold a license to trade with the forbidden city, Lhasa. Their home is in Leh, where the head of the family lives, but they have members in the principal cities with which Leh trades. Two more brothers live at Yarkand and Khotan, respectively, and there is a cousin at Lhasa. In a small way, they are the Warburgs of this part of Asia.

As soon as the Eastern interchange of civilities permitted, we got down to business. At first we were told that the passes would not be open for two weeks, then that perhaps in a week some of our party might start if we would buy ponies, not rent them. By gentle obduracy, however, we finally succeeded in getting away from Leh, not in two weeks or even a week, but in four days, and arranged to rent ponies for all the party.

While we were in Leh a number of entertainments were given for us. These were in the nature of teas with frills. The most interesting was that of the Bahadur Khan. He is a thin, wizened little Punjabi with a long white beard and blue glasses, but he is a good shikary and a real sportsman. We all sat in a row on the piazza of his house. In the garden in front of us a band, consisting of flutes and drums, played whining melodies that all seemed much the same to me. From time to time dancers stepped out from the crowd of people who were watching and danced for us. First came three old women. They wore the native perak, a heavy head-dress of turquoises sewed on cloth extending from a peak on the forehead more than half-way down the back. With it are worn wing-like pieces of black wool that stand out from the ears. The story is that long ago a queen of Ladakh had earache. She thought ear-muffs would help her and had some of this type made. Hence the fashion. These old women did what to me was a very dreary dance. It consisted mainly in hesitant poses and slow shifting of the feet. The natives seemed to enjoy it thoroughly. Then followed native men who performed in much the same manner. The high lights, as far as I was concerned, were a sword-dance and a dance by a Kanjuti. The latter was a fine-looking, light-colored, aquiline-featured man from that race of gallant fighters and stout mountaineers that inhabit the Hunza Valley. He danced with a snap and swagger entirely lacking in the others.

Tea over, we adjourned to the polo-field, where a game was played in our honor. The field was a long, narrow, rather irregular strip of sand. The sides were about five men apiece. I asked of what a team consisted, and was told from four to eleven, so I judge that polo here is like the shinny of my youth, plastic and not cramped with too many rules. Here the Bahadur Khan showed in his proper colors. Stout old sportsman that he was, he turned out in his riding-clothes on a white Balkh stallion and played a good game, white beard, blue glasses, and all. The players ranged from Abdullah Shah, the Aksakal, who played in his fez, to Mongol-looking Ladakhis with pigtails, whose loose robes flapped in the wind as they charged furiously up and down the field. For mounts they had everything from the Balkh stallion, which must have stood fifteen hands high, down to little mouse-like creatures which could have crawled under the average bed without trouble. There was one poor animal that was very lame. Of a necessity, his rider stayed mainly in one place. When the ball happened to come his way he hit it, and the crowd cheered loudly. The best player of the lot was the son of a local Rajah. He rode a little, sausage-shaped pony that galloped like the wind.

The Moravian Mission has been established at Leh for a long time. The members of its staff, Doctor and Mrs. Kunick, and Doctor and Mrs. Asboe, were really fine examples of the practical missionary.

They loved their work and there was never a murmur from them about the hardships they have to undergo. Mrs. Kunick, in particular, was the smooth-browed, courageous, frontier type to which is due in large measure the credit for building our own country.

While we were at Leh, George Cherrie continued his collecting. Every morning at five he was off with his gun. He shot a number of large blue rock-pigeons. They are very good to eat, so after being skinned they were given to Jemal Shah, our cook. Once Cherrie shot a sparrow-hawk, and over my protest turned it over also to the kitchen. When the stew arrived that evening, we could not tell it from the pigeons, and no one to this day knows who ate the hawk.

Saturday, June 6, both our parties started. Cherrie and Cutting, with the larger part of the caravan, went by the winter route where yaks could be used. Kermit and I set out for the Khardong Pass, over which it was reported only coolies could travel. Abdullah Shah, the Aksakal, accompanied our party in order to help in making arrangements beyond the pass. We rode about ten or twelve miles the first day, camping at the foot of the pass at a height of about 15,400 feet. The horses seemed to feel the altitude greatly, and we had to get off and lead them the last part of the way. It was very cold in the stony little nullah where we camped, and our heavy sleeping-bags stood us in good stead.

Next morning we were awake by one o'clock, for that was the time we expected the coolies who were to carry our baggage over the pass. It was cold, but a gorgeous moon was shining and the snow summits that surrounded us seemed quiet and austere. We waited shivering. The coolies did not come. At last about five-thirty we decided they were not coming. There were some yaks belonging to the villagers browsing on one of the slopes near by. We commandeered nine of them, and started as sunrise was flushing rose-pink a few of the highest mountain peaks. We walked ahead. The shaggy black yaks lumbered behind. The first mile or so we scrambled over steep bare rocks. Then we hit the snow-line, and slipped and floundered upward through great drifts. At last we reached the top, 17,800 feet in altitude, higher than either Kermit or I had ever been. The air was really thin and the work of climbing thoroughly winded me. From the top we looked down and watched those who were following us struggling along. Among the first to arrive was old Jemal Shah, the cook. In spite of his gray hair, he stood the work well. Following the men came the great yaks. How they made it, sinking belly-deep in the snow at every other step, I do not see.

As soon as the party had gathered on the crest we started the descent. For those on foot this was moderately easy, though it was over a small snow-covered glacier, but for the animals, carrying from

YAKS CLIMBING THE KHARDONG PASS

A THIBETAN ANTELOPE

160 to 180 pounds apiece, it was very hard work. Again the yaks proved their worth and plodded down without accident.

Kermit and I felt no mountain-sickness when we were on the top of the pass. Curiously enough, however, we developed splitting headaches when we stopped for a rest and something to eat at an altitude of about 16,000 feet. When we camped for the night at Khardong at a height of only 13,500 feet, we really felt we were in the Low Countries.

On the way up to the pass, Kermit had killed a little mountain-rabbit. He chased it over the rocks and finally got it by knocking it over with his khud-stick. It was a chunky little gray animal with crop ears. It would have made an interesting specimen for the museum, and assumed an additional importance in our eyes through the difficulty of its capture. We planned to skin it as soon as we got to camp. When we arrived at the village of Khardong and searched for it through the pockets of Kermit's coat, we could not find it. We decided that it must have fallen out during the climb. It speaks volumes for Kermit's coat that we found it again in those very pockets some ten days later, squashed quite flat from being sat on.

A pathetic instance of the fatalism of the East occurred here. Our two shikaries came from a town in Kashmir named Bandipur. We knew that cholera was raging there and that they were worried about their families. Word reached them via Leh that the daughter and the first cousin of one of them had died. They were naturally heart-broken. In trying to comfort them we suggested that a man be sent back to Leh to send a message to the two families to move to some safer place. To this, Rahima replied sadly: "No, why move them? It is as God wills." We had encountered the "It is Kismet" of the East, to which there is no answer.

At Karthar we were met by Cherrie and Cutting, who had come through safely. At Taghar, one of the little villages at which we camped, we found a ruined palace on the hill back of the town. No one could tell us to whom it had belonged. Probably when the valley was more thoroughly populated some small Rajah had his local seat there. The main building was in fair repair. On one side of the great balcony, which overlooked the surrounding country, there was a partly ruined fresco of Buddha surrounded by various symbolic figures. Below the main palace ruined outbuildings with only the walls standing stretched like a labyrinth over an acre of ground.

At Panamik, where there are hot mineral springs, we had a bath. The natives have a mud bath-house which they use, I am inclined to believe, not so much for cleanliness as because they think the springs have medicinal properties. Farther up the hillside there is a little open basin in which we bathed. The

mineral, I believe, is soda. The bath was a great
luxury, for it was the first hot water we had had
for about four weeks. The overflow from the stream
ran down the hill in a little channel. In the channel
we noticed a green seaweed, about six inches long
and fan-shaped. It was the only water-plant we
saw, for in the cold snow-streams nothing seemed
to grow. Where this weed came from in the high
Himalayas I am not botanist enough to say. Perhaps it survives from some remote period when the
country was totally different geologically.

We were to make the final arrangements for
ponies at Panamik. On our arrival, we went into
the usual Eastern conference, the principals of which
were Kermit and I, Abdullah Shah, our shikaries,
and an amusing old rascal called Shaitan, who owned
the ponies. As usual, "there was a lion in the way,"
and our plans seemed impossible. However, in some
inexplicable fashion, at the end of the second day the
yaks which Shaitan said could not be brought in
from the hills for eight days, were there. The ponies
necessary for the balance of the caravan were to be
produced in another couple of days, and Kermit and
I started ahead for two days' burrhel-shooting.

The burrhel is a member of the sheep family and
lives in the high mountains. He is a little larger than
a donkey. His color is fawn and white, except in the
cases of old males, who have a strong tinge of black.
For any one whose eyes are not trained, he is exceed-

ingly difficult to see, for he blends in with the brown rock and dirt on his native mountainside.

Sometimes we hunted together, sometimes we hunted separately. In addition to our regular shikaries, Rahima and Khalil, we each had a native. These natives were real "jungli wallahs," mountainmen, bred and born in the high Himalayas. They were as tough as old leather. They had eyesight that would shame a telescope. Their clothes were voluminous folds of drab homespun. They ate a curious grain compound. Their skin, garments, and food were all of varying shades of brown.

For the first day's hunt we drew a blank, though we saw quite a number of burrhel. This was due to a combination of long ranges and mediocre shooting on our part.

The second day we started out in different directions. All day I toiled up steep slopes, sometimes slipping on slide rock, sometimes floundering in snow. I saw some cunning little crop-eared rabbits like the one Kermit got on the Khardong Pass. From time to time we saw herds of burrhel, but there were either no large males or we could not get close to them. At last, about six, I came back to camp quite tired. It is one thing to walk all day on the level, and another to climb hills at a height of from 15,000 to 17,000 feet where there is only a hatful of air to go around, and each breath is a gasp. I had not been sitting down more than half an hour, when

Khalil ran up to say that he had just sighted, through the telescope, a herd of burrhel with some good rams near the top of a neighboring nullah. We started at once. On the way out we picked up Kermit, who was just coming in from his hunt. Then the ascent began. It was now nearly dark, so we could lose no time. I must have sounded like a grampus. Kermit, who was making better weather of it, encouraged me once by saying we could not go much higher, as the mountain top was only a short distance away. At last we topped the ridge behind which the animals were feeding, waited a moment to catch our breath, and then advanced. As we reached the last boulders we saw them, a flock of eight rams some hundred yards away. In the gathering dusk it was difficult to judge the size. We picked our animals at once and fired. For a few seconds they were dazed and milled around. Then they made off. Those few seconds gave us an additional opportunity, and two rams dropped dead. We made our way slowly down the mountain in the dark, slipping at every few steps, but satisfied with the evening's work. We got to camp at nine, had some hot cocoa and a drink of brandy which warmed us, and then slept like logs. As so often happens, it was the eleventh-hour effort that got the game.

These burrhel we found in very bad pelage. They were just changing from their winter to their summer coats. When we skinned them the hair came

out in handfuls. They were in such condition that
they would not make proper specimens for mounting in the museum. This confronted us with a very
serious problem, for it was evident that we would
find the poli in much the same shape if we went to
the Pamirs immediately after crossing the Himalayas.
As the poli were to be used for setting up in a group
in the museum, this would never do. We decided,
therefore, to change our plans and to strike directly
for the Tian Shan mountains. On our way back we
could hunt poli, as in late autumn or early winter their
skins would certainly be good.

As Cherrie and Cutting had joined us with the
balance of the pack-ponies, we started next day for
the second great pass, the Sasser. This route has
been used through the ages, and yet it is one of the
most dangerous. It is difficult for the average person
to realize the height of these mountains. The Karakoram Pass, which still lay before us, is more than
19,000 feet, or nearly half again as high as Pike's
Peak. What might be an easy climb at 10,000 feet,
at 17,000 sets the heart beating like a trip-hammer
and the lungs gasping for air. At night it is very
difficult to sleep. You wake every few moments,
struggling for breath, and feel as if you had been
long under water. The severity of the journey is
mutely witnessed by the bones of the pack-animals
which lie everywhere. At many places there are
huge piles six and eight feet high. They are scat-

56

tered and gnawed by the gray wolves of the mountains, which, with the snow-leopards and birds of prey, are the only beneficiaries.

After a hard day's march over glacial streams half covered with ice, and through snow-drifts which pushed right across the valley, we came to our camp at the head of the Sasser glacier. The glacier itself bounded our bivouac so closely on two sides that you could hit it with a stone. On the other sides rose the snow-covered mountains through which we had come by a narrow defile. We were in a natural ice-box. Early in the afternoon the sunshine left us, and an icy breath from the glacier sent the thermometer below freezing. Withal it was very beautiful, for though we were in the shadow, the sun still shone on the encircling peaks whose "silent pinnacles of ancient snow stood sunset flushed."

We pitched no tents that night, but rolled up in our sleeping-bags. The ponies and yaks were kept close together, each beside his load. A few small dung-fires glowed, over which the men cooked their tea. There was little sleep for any of us, as the altitude prevented it. Through the night the men talked and moved around. At one time, Kadi, the Yarkandi, droned a religious chant that went on interminably; a rapidly mumbled monotone of jumbled words punctuated at intervals by a sort of sing-songy chorus. We marvelled that he had the breath to do it. About three-thirty the camp was astir for the day. At the first light, four-thirty, we were under way, for if the sun once thawed the snow-fields on the glacier we would never get over. Once the crust on the snow is melted, the pack-ponies break through and travel becomes impossible. Kermit and I were to shepherd the rear of the caravans. In the faint gray light, we stood and watched the animals, small black dots, climb laboriously up the trail to the top of the glacier. Some fell and had to be set on their feet again. Most of them suffered from the height and had to go slowly. At these heights the ponies should bleed at the nose. If they do not, the men pierce the nostril with a sharp bodkin-like instrument that they carry.

On top was a gently rounded snow-field over which we got without much trouble. Once we had to climb down and up again, where a fissure had separated the ice-field. Here a small black pony fell and could not rise. He carried no pack. He died simply from the height, and was the only casualty of the day. Until seven-thirty we rode down a gradually descending snow slope, when we dropped to a reasonably good trail in the valley, and the glacier was passed. We had played in extraordinarily good luck. The weather had been fine throughout, but we got across none too soon. As the tail of our caravan left the ice a bitter wind arose, snow fell, and a miniature blizzard raged. The camp site lay only a few miles down the valley. When we sat down to a hot breakfast at nine, we were very happy to know that the Sasser was behind us and our caravan safe.

Next day we sent back the yaks we had used over the pass, and started up the Shyok River with our permanent train of slightly over sixty animals. The danger anticipated here was deep water. We had to ford some five times during the day. The first ford was girth-deep, but the ponies took it in fine shape, and all came through. Fezildin, who had charge of the dogs, dragged one across by the collar. After some hesitation the other three, led by Raleigh, the black hound from Mississippi, who was unusually stout of heart, plunged in and swam over. With our caravan were three little donkeys, who, to my surprise, took it as a matter of course, and got through about as well as the larger animals.

Then we headed for the next ford. There was much protest from some of the pony men, but Rahima Loon and the Yarkandi helped to still it. We told them we would follow our usual policy. We would go and look at it. If it were impossible, we would not try it. This ford is around a jutting shoulder of rock and not across the river. When we got there it looked bad. The water was swirling down in a yellow torrent. Even Rahima said: "Bura pani" (bad water). The Yarkandi, however, said he thought it could be done. He got on a horse and tried it. It was just passable and no more. We directed that the horses be led over by ones and

59

twos. The men rolled up their dun-colored clothes
to the waist and plunged in, towing the horses behind them. The water was icy, but neither horses
nor men seemed to mind it. In an hour they were
all safely through. When the last man and horse
struggled out on the beach on the far side, I thought
of some lines from "Kinmont Willie" that mother
used to read me when I was little:

> "The river was spate and full of hate,
> But never a horse nor a man we lost."

From the ford we marched up the trail. It was
gloomy but impressive. There was not even a sprig
of green to rest the eye. On every side rose brown,
rugged mountains that seemed to brood over the
valley. Great glaciers marched down to the very
bank of the stream. Their pinnacled white ice-blocks
seemed like the soldiers of the elder gods. A cold
wind blew fitfully from the snow.

We passed the next fords without trouble. Just
when we thought the worst of the difficulties were
behind us, we turned a bend and saw the Remo
glacier stretched across the entire valley. This was
a very unpleasant surprise. We halted and camped
on the spot. Kermit and I set out at once with a
few men to see if we could find a way across. We
climbed interminably over slippery crags of ice in-
crusted with slime and rocks. Between were deep
crevasses stretching downward until lost in a green-

ish-blue dimness. There was a constant muttering
and groaning. Occasionally some great chunk would
break off and crash down, starting a legion of echoes
that reverberated hollowly through the ice corridors. Some of the men refused to go on, and turned
back. Two hours' fruitless search convinced us that
there was no possibility of getting the ponies across.

This decided, there was but one course open to
us, and that was to return as rapidly as possible and
attempt the other and longer route. Speed was
essential, as the river was rising daily. Moreover,
this delay seriously affected our ponies. Baggage-
animals are scantily rationed while crossing the Himalayas, for they have to carry their own provender.
In addition they lose their strength quickly in the
high altitudes. We knew this mischance would cost
us ponies.

We had to spend the night where we were, but in
order to take advantage of the low period in the
stream before the sun melts the snow and ice, we
started off very early. One by one the chill waters
of the fords were safely negotiated. After the last,
we met two men who were part of the first caravan
of the year from Yarkand, just as we were the first
people to attempt the crossing from Leh. They told
us they had had a bad time. Like us, they had tried
the route down the Shyok River, only to be stopped
by the same glacier. They had stayed there four
days trying to force a way through without success.

As a result one man and eleven animals had died, and they had been forced to eat horse-flesh. They told us, however, that the Karakoram Pass was in good shape.

We pushed on as rapidly as possible and during the next few days passed the Depsang Plain, a bit of barren rolling country 18,000 feet high. A bitter-cold wind swept over it continuously. At last we reached Daulet Beg Uldi, the point from which the Karakoram Pass is usually made. Our ponies had suffered considerably and six more had died. As a result we decided to turn some of the riding-animals into pack-ponies and to use them to relieve those who were weakening. Accordingly, we grouped in pairs the men who had been mounted and assigned one horse to each pair. Kermit and I had one horse between us, and so on.

The approach to the Karakoram was up a long stretch of gradually rising, shale-covered valley. On both sides the trail was lined with the skeletons of dead pack-animals. There were camels, their padded feet sticking stiffly out and patches of skin with brown hair on it clinging to the bones. There were ponies and donkeys in grotesque and hideous positions. There were countless whitened and dis-associated skulls and bones. Overhead three great lammergeyers sailed. Around on rocks were perched coal-black ravens that eyed our caravan with sinister interest. The tracks of wolves were everywhere.

62

On the last steep ascent to the crest of the pass a pack-pony fell off the trail, which brought the number of animals lost to eight. About two o'clock the last of the caravan reached the top and started down the long, gradual slope to the north. "The King of Passes," as one of the shikaries put it, was behind us.

On the Depsang Plain and just beyond the Karakoram the Tibetan antelope range. They are graceful animals, about the size of the American prongbuck which used to live on the plains of our West in millions. They are fawn-colored, dark on the back and almost white on the belly. The male has beautiful tapering horns, sometimes in the shape of a lyre. How they lived in this barren country was a constant source of wonder to us. Their only food seemed to be the sparse tufts of dried grass that were scattered over the surrounding country at very infrequent intervals. They seemed to thrive on this meagre diet, for those we killed were as fat as butter-balls.

The morning after we crossed the Karakoram we saw a herd of seven grazing on our left. They were startled by our approach and fled like shadows across the path of the caravan. I was walking with my rifle at the head. As they went by about 200 yards away I shot and killed the buck and a doe. A little later in the same day Kermit killed another fine buck. This gave us not only our group for the museum but fresh meat.

The fourth of the five great passes, the Suget, we

made quite easily during a twenty-six-mile march. The map we used gives it as 16,610 feet high, but our aneroid made it 18,200 feet, and I am inclined to believe our instrument. All through the country in which we were travelling the maps showed blank areas marked unexplored. The names they gave even to the explored parts were often unrecognized by the natives who used other names. They show nicely marked points which to the uninitiate would mean towns. As a matter of fact, they are nothing but a few fire-blackened rocks where caravans stop, and where no one has lived or ever will. Indeed, in spite of the maps, travelling here is a good deal as described in "The Three Sealers": "Half steam ahead, by guess and lead."

At the end of our march over the Suget we came to grass. It was the first bit of green we had found for nearly nine days. I have rarely seen anything that seemed prettier to me. All the animals were turned out to graze during the evening. Here we had our first visit from the wolves, whose signs we had been seeing all along. During the night one of our three little donkeys was killed and partly eaten by wolves within less than one hundred yards of our camp. None of us heard a sound. I suppose we were sleeping unusually heavily on account of the long march. The next day as we walked down the valley we found it scored not only with the tracks of wolves, but with those of snow-leopards.

In spite of the fact that it was very small and rocky, and would be considered in the United States as almost barren, this valley seemed to us "fair as the garden of the Lord." We had spent nine days in almost total desolation, where the brown rocky stretches were relieved only by patches of snow. The green grass and the tiny sweet-scented spring flowers were to us like a drink of cold water after a long hot trek.

The following day, after a short march, we came to Suget Karaul. It is a square, covering perhaps an acre of ground, surrounded by a mud-and-stone wall with a rampart on top. Inside is a little hut where the Chinese custom officer lives during the summer months. We were too early for him and there was no one at the post. We sent out men to the Kirghiz Begs in order to get some camels to help us over the fords, for the Karakash River was deep. We also needed yaks to assist us over the last big pass, for our ponies were worn out. We armed each man with a note in English, which the Begs could not read, and splendid credentials in Chinese with a gold seal and ribbons given us by the museum, which the Begs could not read either. In a short time a couple of Kirghiz arrived in camp. They were light-colored, wild-looking men who rode camels.

This was the first inhabited country we had seen since we left Panamik. For nearly two weeks we had been travelling through a great stretch of wilderness and mighty mountain fastnesses, which are "no man's land" in every sense of the term.

For the next two days we worked down the Karakash River. It is bordered by scrub thorn-bushes and scant grass. There is practically no wild life. I did not see over a dozen birds in the two days. We struck one really bad ford. It was on a swift-flowing tributary of the Karakash. As usual, it was Kadi, the Yarkandi, who attempted it first. Kermit and I followed right after him, for we felt that once we were on the other side, no argument was possible, the caravan had to follow. We were right, for as we stood on the far shore we could see the men stripping in preparation. Then came the usual shouts, and in they all plunged. One horse fell and was almost drowned, but staggered up and came through after they finally managed to get his pack off.

At the end of the second day we came to a ford before which even stout-hearted Kadi quailed. The water was rough, swift and breast-high. We had to turn aside and go over a mountain ridge instead. Cutting, Kermit, and I scrambled around over the edge of the cliff and waited. It took the train two hours and a half to do about half a mile of map distance. Cherrie, who was with them, said that in all the thirty-eight expeditions he had made, he never saw pack-animals go over so bad a trail. One mule turned five somersaults and got up unhurt.

We camped at Ali-Nazar Kurgan. The town consists of one Kirghiz family, composed of two men and two women. The women were rather pretty, and not at all shy. They were dressed in pink, a rather grimy pink, and wore huge head-dresses shaped like the busbies of grenadiers. They lived in two miserable little caves hollowed out of the dried earth of the hillside. Near by were a few tombs. One of them, evidently that of a well-known chief, was surrounded by horse-heads, burrhel horns, and poli horns. We were much puzzled over the last until we found that the Kirghiz family had brought them when they moved here from the Tagdum Bash Pamirs.

This day's march brought us to our last pass in the Himalayas. During the entire march from Leh, Cherrie collected wherever opportunity afforded. At Panamik, where he stopped for four days, he had obtained not only a number of birds but also two different kinds of rabbits, some mice, and a shrew which he trapped. The birds were moderately numerous until we reached the high altitudes, where there were practically nothing but birds of prey. Our constant companions from the valley of the Sind were a sparrow resembling the English sparrow, a black and rusty brown warbler, the blue rock-pigeon, and the chukor partridge. All of these disappeared when we reached the Depsang Plain. The last two reappeared shortly after the Karakoram Pass. The dividing barriers, as far as bird life is concerned, I should call the Zoji and Karakoram Passes.

Just before we reached the Depsang Plain, we came on a small salt lake in a hollow. On it were at least a dozen ducks. We had no shotguns, so we could not collect any specimens, but we saw them clearly. Their predominating color was light brown, and they were large birds. I believe they were ruddy sheldrakes. A day later, while riding down a barren little mountain stream, Kermit and I flushed five geese. Where the water-birds lived, I cannot say. It did not seem possible that the bodies of water where they were could support them.

After a good night's sleep we got up early and roused the camp for the march on the last pass, the Sanju. This pass, though lower than the others, was more dreaded by our men. It was very difficult to get definite information about it. There were apparently two trails, one very bad on account of a glacier, and the other almost invariably closed at this time of year. Our ponies were all pretty well done up. The grain brought for them by their drivers had given out a couple of days before, and there was nothing for them but grass. We knew they could not get us over. We had, therefore, sent a couple of Kirghiz ahead with fifty rupees to hire fifty yaks to meet us at the foot of the pass and relieve the ponies. This would have settled our worries had we been at all sure the yaks would materialize, but, as

Rahima Loon remarked when discussing it: "Who knows? I give yesterday a Kirghiz four anna to get milk. He get the four anna; I no get the milk." For four hours we marched up a rocky valley, incidentally climbing nearly 4,000 feet. Suddenly, on turning a bend, we saw the yaks before us. There they were, all fifty of them, standing in a group with their drivers. They were a thoroughly welcome sight, for already four ponies had given out. In addition to the men, there was one woman sitting on the hillside. She was evidently the wife of the chief and had come merely "for to admire and for to see." After looking us all over, she mounted a pony and galloped away.

As rapidly as we could we shifted loads and turned to the pass. Fortune favored us and we found the better of the two trails open. This convinced our men that we were under some special providence, as it had not been open this early for fifteen years. Even though better, it was none too good, for it was slide rock and gravel and rose 2,500 feet in a little over two miles. There was, of course, no question of riding ponies, for those poor animals had all they could do to take themselves over, let alone to carry anything. Cherrie rode a yak—the rest of us walked. Kermit and I were by this time thoroughly toughened and acclimated to the altitude, so we went on ahead and waited on the crest for the rest to come. Again I wish to pay tribute to the yaks. They pushed unfalteringly up that hill, carrying 150 pounds or more. At times the slope was at least forty-five degrees. Their tongues hung out and their breathing sounded like the exhaust-valve of a steam-engine, but on they went until one by one they heaved themselves over the last rock and reached the top.

There was a gorgeous view. The mountains on either side were mist-cloaked, and their outlines blurred and softened. Below, zigzagging upward, was the train of more than a hundred animals, and the voices of the drivers, as they shouted, came faintly to us on the gusty wind.

When the train reached the top, we turned to the descent. After a short distance the mist rolled away and we saw spread beneath us rolling green hills. On them were black dots. As we got closer we saw they were flocks of yaks and goats feeding. There were many varieties of bright-colored flowers "star-scattered on the grass." Marmots whistled at us from their holes.

As we rounded a hill we saw some clustered yourts with a group of Kirghiz around them. A yourt is a circular hut with perpendicular walls and a dome roof. Its framework of wood is covered with felt. We went to the principal one, where they were expecting us. Inside there was a fire burning in the centre, over which an old woman and two younger ones were preparing a sort of cruller. Beside it tea was stewing in the usual black-incrusted, pitcher-like copper vessels. The women were dressed in gay colors and had long ribbons hanging down their backs from head-dresses. The room was clean. Around the walls were bridles, cooking-utensils, and a gun with an antelope horn rest to be used in firing. On one side stood a great churn.

We seated ourselves on bright-colored woollen blankets and were served tea, crullers, and some excellent curds. I felt as if I were in the times of Abraham. In a short time the caravan came in safely as far as the men and baggage were concerned, but the last pull had been too severe for four of the ponies. This brought to thirteen the number of animals lost on our twenty-five-day climb over the Himalayas. We had much for which to be thankful, however. Hardly any one had believed it was possible for us to make the journey so early in the season. I know of no other white expedition which has done so. Then there were times when a change in weather or a rise of a few inches in a river would have placed us in a very serious situation. As it was, the Sanju Pass was closed by snow the day after we went through it.

In spite of all this, without the loss of a man or an important piece of baggage we had crossed "the everlasting hills," and were on our way down to the plains of Turkestan.

CHAPTER IV

DESERTS AND OASES OF TURKESTAN

From Ayalik we dropped rapidly to more comfortable heights. Though none of us had really suffered from mountain-sickness, we were glad to be able to take in our quota of oxygen without the labor that had been entailed at the higher altitudes. The principal Mohammedan festival, Muharram, fell upon the second of July, the day after our arrival at Ayalik. All our followers, with the exception of the Ladakhi pony men, were Moslems, so we felt it only just to give them a day to rest and celebrate. This feast corresponds to our Christmas. It happened to be a peculiarly raw and blustering day, so next morning the change was doubly welcome when we dropped down 3,500 feet and camped near two poplars, the first trees we had seen for eighteen days.

There now came up one of the customary debates regarding the trail. The direct route continued to follow the course of the Sanju River, but it was held by some that the waters were too high for the fording involved, and that the alternate road taking two days longer and necessitating the crossing of a fair-sized pass offered the only logical route. We decided on the shorter and more watery trail, and in the way of fords it left nothing to be desired. There were sixteen; all were rapid and rocky and almost all were very deep. At the second, we nearly lost a pony, for one went under and seemed to prefer to stay there, poor beast. He was salvaged against his will, however. Thereafter our lucky star shone forth, for a caravan of twenty unladen camels put in an appearance, and to them we transferred as much weight as they could handle. The camels with their long legs easily crossed fords that would have proved serious obstacles to our heavily laden ponies. With their reduced burdens, the ponies successfully negotiated the remaining fourteen passages and landed us in Sanju amid a lovely grove of willow-trees.

I have always taken particular delight in trees, especially in the old patriarchs of the forest, but to thoroughly appreciate them, one must have spent some weeks in as barren and inhospitable a country as the high Himalayas. It seemed impossible to sufficiently feast our eyes upon the first shady groves at Kivas and Sanju Bazaar.

The day of many fords happened to be the Fourth of July, so that evening in honor of us Jemal Shah called forth his undoubted culinary talents and we feasted and celebrated in orthodox fashion, calling to mind those boyhood Fourths when armed with a plentiful supply of firecrackers we would slip out in the dark hours to disturb the sleep of long-suffering neighbors.

73

Next day, on entering the wide-spread Sanju Bazaar oasis, we were met by a committee of leading citizens—old men with long flowing beards. Greeting our followers, they took both hands of the individual between their own, and then loosing them, each man stroked his own beard, muttering the appropriate formulas of welcome. We were led to a dais covered with carpets and felt numdahs, where food was spread before us; roast lamb and chicken in wooden platters, bowls of curds, plates of nuts and raisins, and basins of apricots and mulberries. Having only recently finished a substantial breakfast, we were not able to do justice to the meat courses, but our treatment of the fruit more than made up for the scant courtesy shown the meat. The camp that night was pitched in a garden of apricot-trees, out of which we shook the fruit. We trooped down to the river to bathe and found the water warm, a pleasant change from the frozen dips with which we had hitherto satisfied our craving for a modified form of cleanliness.

We now abandoned the river and struck across country toward Karghalik. Once out of the oasis, the sun was blistering. For sixteen miles there was no drop of water. We gave the contents of our canteens to the two dogs that were with us, but, in spite of all, we paid toll to the sun in the dog we could least spare, old Foxie. The sudden drop from the freezing altitudes to the blazing lowlands had severely taxed all of the dogs, and Foxie, being the oldest, had suffered more than the others. Every one had become fond of the gallant old fellow, and there was a very genuine mourning in the camp at his death. We buried him in a little garden near the caravansary at Koshtagh, 12,000 miles from his Montana home.

In three days we covered more than eighty miles on our march across to Karghalik. At each oasis we were welcomed with apricots and curds and great flaps of unleavened bread. On our departure, a group of notables would escort us a mile or so on our way. Their mounts were usually stallions, and they formed a vicious, squealing, kicking cavalcade. There was once the start of a fair fight, but none of this appeared to distrub a whit the serenity of the riders.

One morning when we were leaving our night's stopping-place under just such an escort, a big mare that I was riding reached the bridge over an irrigation ditch at the same time as a diminutive pack-pony. Neither wished to yield precedence, but the laden pony was the more adroit, and before I knew what had happened, I was in the ditch. Both the mare and I plunged head under, for the water was deep. No damage was done, although for a moment I was afraid the zeal of the escort in their efforts at rescue might prove my undoing. I had on me my kodak and my Sept, and was much concerned as to their condition. Fortunately, both responded to prompt drying.

At Bora, the last halt before Karghalik, there were two handsome golden eagles in large wooden cages. The townsfolk use them for coursing jeron, the so-called goitred gazelle. They are said to be fairly common on the plains near by during the winter months, but with the advent of summer they retreat into the foot-hills.

Our guides from Bora to Karghalik were four old men mounted upon diminutive donkeys. They rode along in a row, their long beards waggling as they chatted and joked. Sometimes one would ride with his arm on another's shoulder—old cronies evidently.

The Amban of Karghalik had not expected us so soon, and we were thrust upon him in the midst of a levee of local Begs. He was short and squat and cheerful, but language was a distinct barrier and interpreting complicated. He did not speak even Turki, so all sentiments had to be transmitted through Hindustanee, then into Turki and Chinese. Doubtless their outlines became somewhat hazy in the process. We had hoped to avoid stopping over a day, but this proved to be impossible, for the Amban had set his heart upon giving us a tamasha— an entertainment.

In preparation for this affair, we wended down to the rushing yellow river that ran near the garden in which we were camped. A large and intent audience of both sexes watched us bathe. Three of us in our modesty kept on our clothes—they badly needed a wash—but one paid no more attention to the audience than if it had not existed, and has probably joined the galaxy of country deities. Thoroughly washed, we proceeded to dig out tuxedoes and opera-hats, much to the delight of our men, for in Leh they had felt crestfallen at our wearing only workaday clothes.

The Amban arrived early to call for us. We were not ready, so he, his two sons, and entire retinue joined our own men in watching us dress. They were all greatly impressed—so much so that next morning the Amban sent his tailor armed with bundles of black-and-white striped silk. He squatted under a big tree near by busily copying the tuxedoes, while the Amban's carpenter copied our roorkee chairs. The collapsible opera-hats were, alas, quite beyond emulation.

The Amban's dinner was a great success. We had brought with us a small supply of brandy and different sorts of liqueurs to be used as gifts. On such occasions as this we mixed up a palatable cocktail with fruit-juice, brandy, sloe gin, and cherry brandy. On the dinner-table there were two bottles, one held a red liquid, the other a yellow. On the labels were Chinese girls, and beneath were written "Girl Brand Orange Champagne" and "Girl Brand Rose Champagne." It is not so easy to describe the taste. The Amban's two sons were at the dinner—pleasant fellows both. In spite of the lack of a common language, everything went off smoothly, and the Amban seemed particularly to enjoy Cutting's songs. They spoke an international language.

We had decided that we could make better time by travelling at night, so we arranged for several mapas and arabas to be ready after dinner. A mapa is what is known in northern China as a Pekin cart. It is a two-wheeled covered vehicle. An awning stretches out in front to protect the horse. An araba is larger and more primitive. If it has a cover at all, it is only a length of reed matting arched across it. Both have an entire absence of springs. We each crawled into a mapa and stretched out as nearly at full length as possible. A swarm of bobbing Chinese lanterns accompanied us through the darkened bazaar. They never failed to remind me of a Japanese print as they flitted along in the dark. Just outside of town we found the Amban. He had his rugs spread out in the courtyard of a little house at the roadside, and here we alighted for a parting cup of tea with the inevitable accompanying dishes of nuts, raisins, watermelon-seeds, and variegated colored candies. It is a pretty Chinese custom to speed the parting guest on his way by installing oneself at the wayside where the road leaves town, and bidding him alight for a farewell cup of tea.

To sleep soundly in a mapa calls for more than an easy conscience. The ponies are festooned with bells, the ill-fitting wooden joints creak and groan, there is no semblance of a spring, and, to add to all, the driver sings or rather shouts out endless monotonous epics. These he checks from time to time to warn his ponies of some peculiarly bad spot in the road. This warning soon assumed a fateful ring in our ears, and we would grab at any available portion of the wagon's anatomy to mitigate the force of the shocks which inevitably followed.

Up to now, there had been but little travel on the roads we traversed. Occasionally a small caravan had passed us on its way to Ayalik, where the traders were massing preparatory to the first push across the passes. We had come over far in advance of the legitimately open season, and the only caravan which we met en route was the small and sadly decimated one which we passed on the Shyok River. Now, however, we constantly met little groups of men trudging along with laden donkeys or well-fed pack-ponies in tow. From Karghalik on, we never passed out of sight of cultivation of some sort.

We reached Yarkand after marching two nights and part of one day. We were met by the present Amban, two former Ambans, and the Chinese general in command of the troops. All showed us every courtesy. We made our formal calls upon them that afternoon, riding from residence to residence dressed in our state uniform of tuxedo and opera-hat, which always lent a cheerful note. The Aksakal we knew well by name, for he was Abdul Hamid, brother of our friend Abdullah Shah at Leh. We were quartered a couple of miles from town in a large house set in the midst of a most attractive garden. Here we saw our first goitred gazelle, a handsome buck. In his neck he had a swelling that pulsated as he breathed, and reminded one of a well-developed Adam's apple. He was bad-tempered, and when Cherrie in his anxiety to get a good picture motioned the man who was holding him to loose him, he charged straight at the camera with a savage grunt. We came on another pet gazelle later on at a village named Ak-Dong on the Yarkand-Maralbashi road, but this second gazelle had a most pleasant and friendly disposition.

A little while before reaching Karghalik, we had begun to notice cases of goitre, and these increased steadily in frequency until in Yarkand it seemed as if every other person was afflicted. Even small children of four and five had pronounced goitres, and some of their elders had them fearfully developed. It is said to come from the filthy water that the townsfolk drink. A few days out on the Maralbashi road put us beyond the goitre belt, and at Maralbashi I saw only one case. Any one wishing to study the disease would find an unsurpassed field in Yarkand.

We were surprised at the small number of Chinamen we met. A few of the larger stores were run by them, and they seemed to have a monopoly on the pawn-shops, but numerically they were only a small part of the community. It is a land of exile for them. The Amban told us that Pekin was distant six months' travel. The private soldiers were all Yarkandis; occasionally the corporals were Chinese. The natives varied greatly in color; some were as white as we, and others very dark. We saw no negroes nor could we make out any trace of negro blood. The features were not Mongol; as a whole perhaps more Semitic in caste than anything else. The men were better-looking than the women.

We spent three days in Yarkand, making the bundobust for the next stretch of our journey—that to Aksu. I wandered all through the bazaars. There were three separate ones, all extensive. I saw little of European manufacture. Matches and cigarettes were of Chinese make—the cutlery was mostly made upon the spot. I picked up an old pair of Chinese glasses for a friend, and a plate and some other small objects of jade from Khotan, which is a great jade mart. Bazaar life is always interesting and I could watch indefinitely the silversmith, the blacksmith, or the shoemaker at work, or the activities of the bakeshop. In one of the bazaars there was a shrine to some very holy man, with a centrepiece composed of the largest pair of ovis poli horns that I have ever seen. I had no measuring-tape with me, but they must have been almost sixty inches in length measured round the curves.

At Yarkand the expedition split. Suydam went

with Feroze to Kashgar to look after our arrangements there, while Cherrie planned to come slowly on to Maralbashi, stopping a week or more whenever he found a locality where the opportunity for collecting seemed good. Suydam was to join him when he finished at Kashgar, and both were to meet us in the Tekkes around the middle of September.

Ted and I hired six arabas, and shortly after midnight on the 14th of July we piled ourselves and our belongings in them and set out with all the speed feasible for Aksu. We loaded the carts lightly, and hoped to make long marches. Besides Rahima Loon and Khalil, we took with us the second cook, Rooslia, with Loosa and Sultana. Sultana had received sad news at Yarkand. In a letter to Rahima from Bandipar he heard of the death of one of his children, a boy of fourteen. The ravages of cholera had been frightful—more than 700 of the villagers had died. Our Kashmiris reminded me of the crew on a New Bedford whaler in the old days, when almost every member was related by marriage or blood. This of course made it sadder still for the Kashmiris, as each one had a relative or close friend to mourn.

We had become much attached to our followers. Ahmed Shah, who was to take charge of Cherrie's caravan, had proved himself most efficient on the trail across the passes. Feroze was an excellent little fellow; he had a keen sense of humor, and was a merry companion.

Our Kashmiris were a patriarchal group, well led
by Rahima Loon. To his many other qualities, he
superadded that of diplomacy. A born diplomat, he
managed to be ever smoothing our way, and yet
getting us along with amazing speed, for which he
fully realized the necessity. He watched over the
finances with an eagle eye, and time and again
saved us many rupees. Not only did he cut down
the larger expenditures, but he also kept well under
control the small daily sums that have such a tendency to mount.

Jemal Shah, the veteran cook, we left with Cherrie.
He had come through everything smiling, and had
conjured up the most magnificent meals from nowhere, when confronted by what seemed a hopeless
insufficiency of time and materials. Just as the
arabas were about to start into the black night, he
ran up and presented us each with a box of matches
as a final precaution for our comfort.

The Kashmiris were adepts in the art of massage.
All Asiatics are firm believers in it. In the bazaar
at Maralbashi I came on a Darby and Joan picture
—an old woman massaging the feet of her white-
bearded husband. I was once much indebted to this
massage on the way across the passes. While running to adjust a load, I slipped on a stone and threw
my knee out so severely that I was for some time
unable to put the slightest weight on it. Rahima
massaged it night and morning for several days with

83

ghee—rancid native butter—and I was back in walking trim much sooner than I had dared to believe possible. All our followers were most concerned and considerate, and at odd moments would take a turn at massaging the knee. Kadi, the Yarkandi, also tried his hand. They practised both massage and osteopathy upon each other for every ailment from a headache to a stomachache. To cure this latter, Suydam saw one of the men lying face down on the ground while the others beat his arms and legs in a truly alarming fashion.

At Yarkand we parted with Kadi and his two partners, who had come with us from Leh. All three wished to continue on to the Tian Shan, but Rahima felt that they would be out of their bailiwick and of little use. We had become genuinely attached to Kadi, he was so everlastingly cheerful and hard-working. Short but beautifully proportioned, he had in his walk that resiliency you so often see in a well-conditioned hunting-dog. All day long he would be hurrying from one end of the column to the other, adjusting the loads here and there, helping a fallen pony to regain his footing, and yet coming into camp at night after the longest day's march his step would be as springy as if he were but setting out. He was invaluable at the fords, always the first across, returning time after time to help the others over.

The stretch from Yarkand to Maralbashi we made in six days, averaging better than twenty-two miles.

THE FAIR AT YARKAND

FERRYING ACROSS THE YARKAND RIVER

At the start we tried night marching, but as there was no moon, the combination of bad roads and evening rain-storms made us feel it preferable to put up with the heat of the sun. The Amban of Yarkand had been most efficient in sending ahead word to the villagers to help us along. He was a keen-faced, slightly built man, evidently accustomed to act quickly and be obeyed. He warned us that much of the road was under water and that we might find ourselves in difficulties, but promised to give us all assistance possible.

We crossed to the right bank of the river at Toghraghe, fifteen or sixteen miles from Yarkand. This was a slow performance, for the river was very broad, with two deep channels, separated by a mud flat, where the carts had to be unloaded and hauled across by the horses. Next day we began to get out of the cultivated districts, and passed through a jungle of dwarfed poplar-trees. It looked as if there should be game about, but the natives insisted that there was none. It had rained, as usual, during the night, and at sun-up the air was delightfully clear. We had a brief glimpse of the Kuen Lun mountains behind us, bounding with their glorious snowy peaks the southern horizon. It is only on rare occasions that you can see any distance, for the fine desert dust that has been whirled about by the wind remains suspended in the air and effectively restricts one's vision.

On the third day after starting from Merket Ba-

zaar we crossed back to the left bank of the river,
following a jungle trail which had been widened and
vastly improved for us at the command of the Amban. We had with us two Yarkandi soldiers, one of
them an efficient picturesque fellow, a local proto-
type of Dugald Dalgetty. Somewhere he had acquired a black slouch-hat, and in a bickering had
lost a good part of one ear. He was death on straggling, and after one or two fruitless attempts at
apathetic resistance, our araba drivers spruced up
and kept in close formation. Our soldier was no
believer in Gandhiism.

We had with us both Cumberland's and Church's
accounts of their hunting trips in Turkestan. We
found Major Cumberland's the best reading of any
of the books on the country. There is no question
but that there is far less game now along the trail
from Yarkand to Aksu than there was when he
was here in 1889; less, too, than when Church was
through, ten years later. The local shikaries told us
that it was too hot and dry at this season, July, but
that in another two months the game would return.
Such is, without doubt, the case. Still, where Cumberland mentioned not once but many times running
across the fresh trail of tiger, we could not even hear
from the natives of there being tigers in the neighborhood. They would have been only too glad to en-
large upon any such information had there been the
slightest foundation on which to build.

86

On the Yarkand side of Maralbashi the villages
of Aksakmaral and Shamal are supposed to be the
best centres from which to hunt. Beyond Maralbashi on the Aksu road, Yakka Kudak is regarded
as the most likely place for shikar. We were going
through with all possible speed, but whenever the
local oracles gave us the slightest encouragement, we
took ponies and got in an early morning's hunt,
catching the arabas at noon. We separated, one
taking Rahima and the other Khalil, with, of course,
a local so-called shikarry (save the mark!) in addition. Each time that we went out, either one or
both of us caught a fleeting glimpse of gazelles.
There was never a chance for a shot, however, for
they were wild as hawks. We saw but very little recent sign, so the place or time was wrong, probably
both.

Of other wild life there was not a great deal. During a morning's hunt I counted over a dozen hares.
Aside from that day, we never saw more than one or
two. Duck and geese were plentiful in some of the
lagoons and often amazingly tame. Of the pheasants
about which Cumberland and Church wrote, we saw
not one. The sole contribution we made to our
collection was a brown snake about eighteen inches
long which a native brought in. This was the only
snake, dead or alive, which we had seen on the whole
expedition up to date.

As a rule, we had been sleeping in the dirty bat-

tered caravansaries of the villages where we halted,
When we came in late this was a necessity. Whenever it was possible to find a garden near by, we
either had our tent up or laid our sleeping-bags on
the ground uncovered, if the night gave promise of
being fine.

Rough and uncertain as was the road, we were
travelling along what has been a trade route through
countless generations. Marco Polo may well have
put up in more than one of the serais in which we
stopped. These serais are big courtyards lined on
either side with stalls for cattle, having a number of
large rooms in the rear for use of travellers. Outside
of these rooms are earthen daises on which we un-
rolled our sleeping-bags. Sometimes there would be
other travellers in our serai, and the different groups
would squat over their cooking-pots, plunging their
hands into the communal dish. The evening meal
over, they would sing spirited ballad songs with a
swinging lilt to them or lugubrious dirges and in-
describably monotonous chants.

After dark there was much of the glamor of the
East to be enjoyed in the serai and its assemblage,
which by daylight was obscured by raw ugliness and
filth. The night-watches were not always peaceful,
for more often than not the fleas bit shrewdly. Once
we were set upon by some peculiarly large and savage bug whose attack became only the fiercer the
more Keating's powder was strewn about "and him

as big as a donkey," at least so it seemed from the wounds inflicted. Suydam on that occasion fared the worst, for his bites swelled and started to fester. It may be understood, therefore, why we preferred our unromantic tents to the age-old serai.

It was always difficult, however, to persuade our men to go on beyond the well-known halting-places. The drivers and our guides were very conventional, and to go past a regulation stage never seemed to them possible. It was not that wood and water and other necessities were not available at any number of places. It was just that these definite places have been the stages time out of mind, and custom ordains that there be no deviation. Then, too, for some reason the men regarded the serai as more fitting and dignified.

The village musicians usually gathered in the serai. An average band consisted of a stringed instrument with a body no larger than a mandolin's but the stem a good six feet long, a couple more stringed instruments only half as large, and one or two tambourines. Sometimes the musicians sang, sometimes not—and often a man would jump up and dance. Music is a profession not much more highly considered in Yarkand than in Ladakh, where the musician ranks lower than the blacksmith or tinsmith—indeed, he is almost the lowest class of all.

The best dancing that I saw was in Karghalik. The men having performed at the Amban's levee were afterward gathered in a secluded spot in the garden under some apricot-trees. They started again for their own amusement and there I found them, and enjoyed their dancing more than I had at the tamasha. One man would dance for a while, and then he would select another from the surrounding circle, and hale him out. They covered their hands with their long sleeves just as one sees in the jade statue of a Kien Lung dancing-girl. Occasionally an onlooker would step forward with some money in his hand, pass it a couple of times around the dancer's head, and then put it in an idle tambourine that lay beside the musicians.

At Maralbashi, which we reached on July 19, we again unearthed our worn and weary tuxedoes, and, topped off with opera-hats, returned the Amban's call, mounted on two ambitious ponies. We succeeded in hurrying through without waiting over the usual day. We left on the afternoon following our arrival, first having lunch with the Amban and two other Chinese officials. If we had been able to speak Chinese, these luncheons would have been both pleasant and interesting, but as it was, the only thing we could do without the aid of an interpreter was to pledge each other in Chinese brandy. In some way a pint of champagne had found its way here, and it was produced in our honor. It had been flat for many years and we drank it as a liqueur.

The Amban was courtesy itself, and sent on two

soldiers to take the place of those that came with us from Yarkand, also two local Begs to see that we had our wants supplied in the villages through which we passed. We had brought with us some brandy and various kinds of liqueurs to be sent as presents to the Ambans. We greatly regretted that we had not also thought of wrist-watches, for they would have served admirably as gifts.

The bazaar of Maralbashi is one long street, lined with the usual bake-shops, butcher-shops, and all the other shops with their display of gimcracks of every kind. There were many birds in cages, seemingly more than in any bazaar through which we had yet passed. The red-legged chukor appeared a favorite. There were also quail, desert larks, and finches. One morning on the road we met a troupe of six donkeys. On one was a man with a fat small boy perched in front of him, on another was his wife, while strapped on each of the other four were bobbing along four birds in their cages.

The donkey is much used as a conveyance. The rider has stirrups but no bridle, and guides his charger by hitting him on one side or other of the neck, uttering inimitable guttural sounds. It is surprising what heavy loads of grain a donkey will carry. When you see them coming along under a load of brush it looks as if "Birnam wood had come to Dunsinane."

Our araba drivers had needed urging on the road to Maralbashi, when they often wished to stop short of our proposed day's march. They had also tried to persuade us to stay over there on the plea of sick horses. Now they had apparently made up their minds that the best thing to do was to hurry through to Aksu and get rid of us, for they made amazingly good time of their own accord. We were only six days on the road, averaging twenty-four miles a day. When a driver wishes to shorten a stage, he will plead that there is no grass nor wood on the road ahead, or that there is too much water—sometimes all three. Then if you have halted in response to his petition, you will probably next morning find that there were a dozen good places farther on to have camped, and no lack of wood or fodder, nor superfluity of water. The driver will be entirely unabashed when you point this out with some acerbity, and with a childlike faith he will offer the same time-honored reasons when next the occasion warrants.

Our horses were excellent, all of them stallions, and in fine shape. They did not seem to lose condition on the road, but of course they had an abundance to eat. An araba is drawn by from one to four horses, according to the load or the fancy of the driver. We had two with one horse only, three with one horse in the shafts and another in front, tandem fashion, and one with three horses. The wheel-horses were most intelligent. They would back into place between the shafts merely at the spoken word, and they would shift to right or left on the road at their driver's command. There were no reins. A single rope was attached to the bit of each horse, but it was rarely used.

Although an araba is not a comfortable conveyance for man, we unquestionably made better time and at far less expense than we could have done with a pack-train. Our six arabas took us nearly 300 miles for about eighty-five dollars. We would have needed fifteen pack-ponies. We had one araba for the dogs—they could never have got through the long hot marches on foot, and we particularly wished to fatten them up for the hunting. They had, of course, got very thin during the trek across the passes, but soon began to put on weight and cover their ribs. In the arabas we either lay on our bedding-rolls or sat tailor fashion upon them. When the road was sandy we read for a while, but our eyes tired and an ear had to be kept open for the "Oowah! Oowah!" with which the drivers encouraged their teams across the particularly rough spots in the road. Then we clutched any part of the araba and held on, while the cart bucketed and swayed its way along. Ted put in most of his time on the Bible and Shakespeare, while I had a more varied diet— three plays of Molière, Lever's "Handy Andy," and "Westward Ho!"

There was more waste land on the Aksu road. For two days in the neighborhood of Yakka Kudak we passed through almost continuous desert. Once for several miles the whole surface of the land to a depth of eight feet had been bodily removed and deposited elsewhere by the wind. Numerous hummocks, held together by roots of the dead trees perched on the summit, attested to the former earth level and gave the place an eerie and ghostlike appearance—seemingly an abode of the dead.

Whenever we had the slightest encouragement from the natives, we went off in search of gazelle, but without success. When planning the expedition, we had felt that to bring any shotgun other than Cherrie's collecting guns would involve too serious an addition of weight. For a while, we thought of a .22 rifle, but decided against it as not being worth the trouble. We would have been glad of the .22 many times when we could have used it on chukor, duck, or rabbit. What we really should have taken along was a .410 pump-gun. The shells are light and it would have been powerful enough to serve our wants. On an expedition of this sort all you require is weapons to shoot specimens and provide for variation in the diet. We had no desire for sporting wing-shooting, but wished to bag our game with the least expenditure of powder. Sixteen or twelve gauge shells weighed so much as to be out of the question for us.

Five or six miles before reaching Yangi Shahr, we crossed the Aksu River. Here we halted to wash off the dust of travel—and looking at the water it seemed doubtful whether we would wash more off or on.

After our swim we dressed as usual in evening clothes and opera-hats. We sent the arabas on and arranged for riding-ponies. We always felt like waiters in a very second-class restaurant, but unquestionably these clothes served a good purpose, for the officials felt that, dirty or not, the intention to do honor was there. A business suit would not have meant the same thing, but the military uniforms that we had for a time considered would have done admirably.

During the ride in, we realized that we were once more in the goitre belt. In Aksu it was not as prevalent as in Yarkand, but it seemed to be more virulent, and the cases more advanced. The little babies were a sad sight.

A lovely garden had been prepared for us, the best-kept one which we had yet come upon. Carpets and numdahs were spread, and on tables were fresh and dried fruits, together with the usual nuts, raisins, and sugar candy. The muskmelons were delicious, and here we first were given watermelons. The apricot season was over. There were peaches, small but good, and a glossy red fruit, a cross between apricot and peach, which didn't appear to be ripe, although every one ate it. There were grapes of different varieties, but all were green as yet.

Yangi Shahr is the Chinese city of Aksu—lying about five miles from the native city. In Yangi Shahr the Dotai, or Governor, of the province resides, as well as the Lieutenant-Governor and the local

Amban. Each had some species of European carriage, ranging from a fiacre to a Russian troika on wheels. The latter was sent to convey us to the Dotai's residence, where we sat through an innumerable coursed dinner, while some itinerant Chinese players shouted and sang and danced near by. There appeared to be no plot, but part of the buffoonery was easily understood and appreciated.

The Dotai was a big, jovial man. Had we had a common language we should have thoroughly enjoyed the time with him, but he was a "brother hedged by alien speech and lacking all interpreter." Our men spoke a very halting Turki, therefore we had another added temporarily to the string of interpreters—a man who fancied he was able to understand our men's Turki and translate it to his fellows. Ted compared the whole arrangement to the game of gossip that we used to play as children. One child would whisper a sentence to another, he to still another, and so on, until it rounded the circle and came back to its originator, who shouted out what he had first said, and in what form it had returned to him. The comparison enabled us to form some idea of how much of what we said seeped through to the Dotai. The Dotai was an efficient executive, he made up his mind quickly, and acted immediately. When he told us arrangements for our march into the Tekkes would be completed without delay, we felt there was no question but that such would be the case, and we had nothing to worry about.

After a night in Yangi Shahr, we moved on to Aksu to complete the arrangements for pushing on across the Muzart Pass into the valley of the Tekkes, for we were eager to reach the promised land of big game.

CHAPTER V

BEYOND THE LAST BARRIER TO THE PROMISED HUNTING–GROUNDS

"But the land whither ye go is a land of hills and valleys, and drinketh water of the rain from heaven."

—DEUTERONOMY 2 : 2.

AT Aksu we stayed a couple of days, for here we had to change from arabas back to pack-ponies for our trip through the Tian Shan mountains. We did not enjoy ourselves, as we were impatient to be off. It was swelteringly hot in the Amban's garden where we were camped. During the day flies swarmed over everything like the Egyptian plague, and at night the mosquitoes descended on us in armies. The Amban all but killed us with courtesy, calling about every two hours. We eventually curtailed his calls by letting loose our hounds. The bright spots in our stay were some lovely old embroidered robes and some quaint bits of china that we picked up. Aksu is a very old town, so far off the beaten road that it has not been swept clean of its treasures.

On the morning of our departure all was bustle and confusion. The new pack-ponies had just come in from the range. They were grass-fed, pot-bellied, and full of spirits. Packing them was difficult. Often a pony half laden with yakdans and boxes would squeal, plunge and buck across the court-yard, towing a yelling Turki behind him and scattering camp utensils in all directions. Girthing up a pack-pony in this country is a remarkable procedure. A man gets on either side, the pack is put on, then each man places a foot against the pony's side and pulls the pack-ropes with every ounce of strength he has. Every time I saw it done I expected the animal to be cut in two like Baron Munchausen's famous horse.

The train packed, we marched out of town. We were preceded by a platoon of soldiers with fixed bayonets. Their rifles were nearly fifty years old, and their uniforms were original, to say the least. As we pushed through the bazaar we collected an additional escort of dozens of little boys. Like boys the world over, they gathered thick as flies around the marching column. They darted in front of the horses, under their very noses, and I was afraid our collections in this part of China would start with a Turki boy. Just beyond the town the Amban was waiting. We said good-by. The soldiers presented arms, and our escort left us.

In a short distance our road turned up the side of the steep white clay cliff that bounds the Aksu Valley. Our way lay through a deep cut, worn by generations of travel. As we plodded up, the day, which had been overcast, suddenly cleared, and a brilliant sun shone. We turned a corner and saw at the top of the rise, silhouetted against the clear blue of the sky, a white-domed mosque with a fretted wall. It was surrounded by gently waving green poplars, and was set like a picture by the tall white banks on either side of the road. Every shadow was diamond-cut by the bright sunlight, every line was clear in the clean air. It was a fairy scene from the "Arabian Nights."

On the top of the cliffs a broad flat plateau stretched for miles. It was dotted in every direction with Moslem tombs. Arches, domes, squares, and walls of white-baked clay were scattered in a seemingly endless succession. An occasional tree gave a dash of color. We looked beyond, and there to the north, hanging like clouds on the horizon, were the snowy peaks of the Tian Shan mountains —our promised land.

For three days we journeyed northeast across the plain. It was a great relief to be riding again after the ceaseless jarring of the arabas in which we had been driving. During the second day we made a fruitless attempt to get a gazelle. We saw quite a number, but the plain was very flat and they were very wary. They generally saw us before we saw them, so our hunt consisted in the main of watching them through field-glasses as they disappeared with great graceful bounds. As we were anxious to reach the Tian Shan as soon as possible, we had to abandon the hunt for the present.

At Khurgan we struck the foot-hills, and camped for the night. A wind off the snow blew down the valley. We were cool for the first time in nearly a month. This place gets its name from the Chinese fort there. Khurgan is Turki for fort. Like all Chinese forts I have seen, it is an emblem of authority rather than a military weapon. It consists of a mud-walled square and a rampart running across the valley from the river. An active boy could climb up the near-by hill and throw stones into the fort itself. It was garrisoned by three Chinese customs officials. One of them was a remarkable old fellow. He was the father-in-law of the Aksu Amban and could not have been a day under eighty, but he rode out some three miles to meet us and handled his horse with dash and decision.

On August 1 we left Khurgan for our trip up the Aksu Valley to the mountains. Besides our regular train we had with us quite a number of people. The high ranker among these was Ishmael Bey, an important Beg from Kizil Bulak, who handled the traffic north from that town. He was a handsome man, tall and powerful, with fine features and a heavy, grizzled black beard. He wore a fur cap, and a long brown coat caught in at the waist with a bright-colored silk scarf. He rode an excellent horse. More important than all this, he had a stout heart. Time and again he was invaluable in getting the caravan over difficult places. He would go any-

101

where any of the men would, and go first. They told me he was a man of great wealth, and then in true Biblical fashion enumerated his riches: 5,000 sheep, 3,000 goats, 1,000 donkeys, 300 ponies, and 30 camels —literally "the cattle on a thousand hills." He had with him a number of his servants, dark-skinned, black-bearded men. Two of them carried ancient flint-lock rifles. The Beg himself had a single-shot Russian army rifle of the 1876 model. Each of these rifles had a pronged rest near the muzzle, which was let down when the piece was fired.

There were also a number of other Begs who had come over the pass to meet us. With one of them were his wife and son. The woman was dressed in riding-clothes like a man. The conventionalities were satisfied by a little white curtain fastened to the front of her cap, which she let down over her face at the halts. On the march she did not bother about it. She had a jolly brown wrinkled face, much like a walnut. The boy was about twelve and rather fresh and obnoxious. He rode well, however, and had plenty of courage. Our party was completed by two Chinese soldiers attached to us as a guard of honor. We would have liked to get rid of them, but they stuck to us like burrs. I am inclined to think that the bukshish we gave them was about the only pay on which they could count. One of them was almost white, with gray eyes. I believe he must have been half Russian, though I could never find out, as he spoke only Chinese. The other was a picturesque old Oriental. He looked like an elderly serious monkey, and rarely changed his expression. He was very thin, and his nondescript uniform hung around him like a flag around a flagpole on a windless day. He carried a long-stemmed pipe with a little bowl, and a black horsetail fly-brush, and wore what we used to call when we were little a "farmer-hayseed hat."

In the Aksu Valley, for the first time since leaving Kashmir, we found hills where there was regular rainfall. There were patches of grass in the nullahs. The northern slopes got most of the rain. On some of these fir-trees marched "like black priests in a row" to the hill crest. Along the river-bank there was a fringe of trees with grass, ferns and flowers beneath. Above all there was that sense of cleanliness and austerity which only the mountains and great woods give.

Wild life was plentiful. Hare were constantly loping off in front of us. There were numbers of small birds, larks, sparrows, and warblers. Crossing a small meadow we flushed a partridge, the first we had seen. Once we saw an old mother chukor with her young. She did not want to leave them, and they were very little, so we were able to get within a dozen feet of the whole family. The old mother clucked just like any barnyard hen. The little ones were brownish midgets and scuttled very actively through the grass.

We were held up at the end of the first day's march by a bad ford. Ishmael Bey's baggage reached it first. Five loads got over and then the stream rose. When we got there the water was rushing past so deep and swift that no loaded animal could make it. We tried it with an unloaded camel, and almost lost him down-stream. These snow-fed glacier streams rise very suddenly. When the sun shines during the day the streams are swelled by the melting snow and ice. At night when the glaciers freeze again, the water drops. The time of day at which any particular ford is high depends, of course, on how long it takes for the snow-water to reach it. Where the ford is near the glacier the water rises early in the morning and falls early in the evening. Where the ford is far down the river, the rise may not take place until late in the afternoon, and the fall until early next morning. The traveller prays for cloudy weather when he has to do mountain-fording.

Early next morning we were waked by the raucous squealing of the camels that we had collected from the near-by country to help us across the bad fords. The camp was already up. Shortly after light we started the balance of the Beg's baggage over the stream. He had been using donkeys, but now his loads were put on camels. A man got on top of each loaded camel and held two donkeys by very long lead ropes. The camels then proceeded to take the ford, towing the donkeys after them like rowboats after a launch. Following this our baggage went over in the same fashion. Kermit and I followed on our horses. We each took a dog on our saddles, for, as the stream was nothing but rapids, we were afraid they might be drowned. This made riding a complicated matter, as neither dog wanted to stay where it was. To make matters worse, in the middle of the river first one and then the other of the horses stumbled and all but fell. At this point both dogs decided to get off, and what with trying to hold a squirming dog, guide the horse and whip it forward at the same time, all of us very nearly went down the stream.

After we reached the other side our unloaded baggage-animals were herded in, the men riding behind. The horse ridden by one of the men slipped in the middle of the stream, made a desperate attempt to recover itself, and then the horse and man plunged into the rapids. In no time they were whirling downstream like a log in a spring freshet. The man held on to the horse. Over and over they rolled, sometimes one above, sometimes the other. I made an ineffectual attempt to reach them by wading out, but they swirled by before I could get near them. Men on horseback galloped after them down each bank, for the current was carrying them so fast it was impossible to keep up by running on foot. Down they sank in the water. For more than fifty yards I did not see the man at all. At last, more than 300 yards below, they touched one bank. Men were there as soon as they grounded. The horse was dead, but when they rolled it over and pulled the man out from underneath, the man was living. Not only was he alive, but in spite of the time he had been under water, and the rocks against which he had been battered, he had suffered no real hurt.

Troubles never come singly, and sure enough at the next ford we all but lost another man. The caravan was practically over. The Chinese soldier with the straw hat, pipe, and fly-brush was bringing up the rear. Suddenly his horse stumbled, floundered, and both were rolling in the water. Warned by our previous experience, I had taken a position at a point below the ford, near which I thought any man carried down by current would drift. I jumped into the water. Luckily he came close and I grabbed his hand. I was carried off my feet by the current, but Kermit and Rahima Loon arrived on the run, and between us we succeeded in pulling him out. Rahima plunged in without a moment's hesitation, although he cannot swim a stroke. When we got the Chinaman on the bank and emptied some of the water out of him, we found he still had his hat, his fly-brush, and his pipe. Indeed, as far as we could see, even his expression had not changed. He finished the day wrapped up in a poshteen made for a man twice his size, which flapped in the wind, and, combined with his inevitable straw hat, made him look like a dilapidated scarecrow.

This last ducking finished the fording for the day. There is a song about a steeplechase course in Maryland which says that to cover the course successfully "It takes a lean wiry rider on a horse like a spider." Kermit and I agreed that this applied also to the fords of the Muzart River.

Just before the end of the march we saw our first ibex. There were some twenty of them feeding at the top of a high ravine. Against the green they looked like tiny, tawny dots. It was our first glimpse of the game for which we had ridden and walked over the high Himalayas and through the plains of Turkestan.

The shikaries got out the telescopes and, after studying the ibex carefully, told us that there were no good males, nothing with horns measuring over thirty inches. Of course there was no point then in stalking them. When they saw us, they trotted up the nullah in single file. They crossed what looked like an impassable precipice, springing from rock to ledge with apparent ease. The last we saw of them was a row of black dots against the snow on the top of the mountain.

That night saw us camped but half a mile from the foot of the Muzart glacier, at a place called Tango Tash. Like many places, it is merely a name on the map. The camp site was a barren bit of level ground backed up against a great cliff. On this rock natives as they passed had scrawled rude sketches. We

107

recognized ibex, wild sheep, and the figures of men. They were not nearly so good as the Magdalenian drawings. The only wild life we saw near the camp were a couple of very friendly purple finches. They hopped around not ten feet away, waiting for crumbs while we ate supper.

It was raining next morning when we started. We crossed a steep neck of land. Ahead through the mist loomed the glacier, its mass stretched from one side of the valley to the other. As far as the eye could see there were ridges of dirty snow, rock, and débris. We reached the top after a fairly stiff climb, and wound our way around hummocks and boulders for over an hour and a half. The rain now changed into a driving wet snow. We came to a very steep and high ice-cliff. The men cut steps in it by which the pack-animals climbed up. Fully half of the ponies fell at least once. Two or three of them turned complete somersaults which would have killed any of our Eastern ponies. At length they reached the top, all unhurt. Scattered over this glacier and its approaches were the same piles of skeletons of pack-animals that we had found in the Himalayas. Here at the foot of the ice-cliff were the remains of a little donkey, its head wedged in a rock, evidently the victim of a slide.

At the top of the cliff was a family of five Kirghiz who stayed there all the year round and acted as a rescue post. They lived in a square stone building perched on an almost naked shoulder of rock at one side of the glacier. Around it were half a dozen graves. They were mere piles of stone into which poles with horses' tails attached had been stuck. At the base of the poles were heaped the horns of wild sheep and ibex. I could not find out who lay buried there. All my questions brought out were, first, the statement that they were "big men" and, second, the fact that they "died long ago." It was a wild and lonely spot for a graveyard.

Beyond through the snow the glacier stretched in a series of weird shapes. We pushed on past green icy streams that ran down through channels in the ice. We skirted small lakes and crevasses. Once we went astray, and after going nearly a mile out of our way, brought up against a fissure we could not pass. There was nothing to do but grope our way back through the whirling snow. At last after nearly six hours' work, we turned sharp to the west, left the glacier, and crossed over a low ridge which is the pass proper.

The ridge was covered with green turf and was easy going. The snow had turned to rain again, but we were all thoroughly cold and uncomfortable. Five miles farther on we came to a lower valley where a caravan from Kulja was camped. The pony men were squatted under a rude shelter made of bales of wool and blankets. With the ready hospitality of the travellers on lone trails, they gave us hot tea and bread. Our caravan, which had fallen behind, now joined us and we marched on down the valley. Soon the grassy slopes gave way to spruce woods that pushed up the little ravines toward the crests like an invading army. In the valley were green meadows.

We turned a shoulder and came to our camping-ground. It was a broad stretch of grass by the river. On it stood three log huts. They were built much the same as the log cabins of our own West. Their roofs were covered with earth, on which grass was growing. The rushing stream, the snowy mountains, the fir-trees, and the log cabins all made me feel as if I were in the Northern Rockies.

The huts belonged to the Beg with the wife and child. As we approached them a number of men and women came out to meet us, with the usual escort of snarling pie-dogs. We were given a warm welcome. Numdahs were spread and tea, curds, bread, and fresh butter were served us. We did them full justice, especially the fresh butter. The women bustled about and prepared the food for us, with no sign of embarrassment and no attempt to cover their faces.

Shortly after we arrived they started to put up a native tent, or yourt, for us to use. A yourt is circular and dome-shaped, with a diameter of about twenty-five feet and a height in the centre of nearly twelve feet. Considering its size, they built it remarkably quickly. First they brought out a lattice-work of wood, fastened together with leather thongs.

It was collapsible, like the gates on our ferry-boats. They arranged it in a circle. Then a man stood in the centre, holding on the end of a pole a circular bit of wood, like the rim of a wheel pierced with holes. Next the women took long poles, fitted them into the holes in the centrepiece, and lashed the other ends to the latticework. It looked for all the world like some complicated May-pole dance. This completed the framework. Over it they draped great pieces of felt and fastened them with bands of woven horsehair. A hole was left in the middle of the dome for a chimney, and a regular door-frame about five feet high was fitted into a gap in the latticework. The yourt was finished in less than twenty minutes. The floor was covered with soft numdahs except for a place left bare for the fire. It made a most comfortable shelter after our very diminutive tent, or the serais where fleas made the night one continuous desperate battle.

The whole meadow where we camped was covered with bright-colored flowers, as if it had rained confetti. Within forty feet of our tent I picked sixteen different kinds. There were golden poppies like those of California, there were blue forget-me-nots, daisies of all colors, and many others which were like none I had seen before. Last, but not least, there was the good, broad, honest face of the yellow dandelion. The flowers were not confined to this meadow. They were under the trees in the woods and high on the mountains as well. We crossed slopes of shale in the passes where the gray of the rock was only broken by the brilliancy of mats of pansies and violets. Once I came out of a stretch of spruce forest and saw before me a glade literally frosted with snow-white blossoms. I longed for my mother, who loves flowers, knows them, and from whom I learned the very little I know about them.

The evening we arrived we were sitting in the yourt. I had already taken off my wet boots and Kermit was writing letters. Suddenly Khalil ran in very much excited, exclaiming "illik! illik!" the local name for Siberian roe. We were outside in an instant. We found Rahima studying the opposite side of the valley with field-glasses. He showed us where there were two roes feeding just above a grove of trees. They could be seen quite plainly through the glasses. One was a doe, but the other was a nice buck. It was clearly a case where only one man could shoot, so we flipped a coin. I won and hastily put on my wet boots again. Meanwhile the horses were saddled. Khalil, a local man and I cantered off down the stream to the ford. We splashed through the water and rode up the other side as far as we could through the woods. At last it became so thick that we left the horses and went ahead on foot. Both Khalil and the local man went through the under-brush and up the hill like deer. I panted after, calling to them in a hoarse whisper to go more slowly or

when we got there I would be too much out of breath
to shoot. At last Khalil put his head cautiously over
a clump of bushes and beckoned to me. I crept up,
and there about seventy yards away, just vanishing
into a grove of trees, were the two deer. There
was no time to lose, so I shot as quickly as possible
at the buck. By the time I got my rifle up, all I
could see of him was his rump. He went down but
was up again and off in an instant. We ran over to
where he had been, and found a heavy blood-trail.
We followed it in the failing light for 200 yards until
it got too dark to see and we had to give up for the
day. I mounted my horse and rode back to camp
very disconsolately, for I hate leaving a wounded
animal. It was nearly nine o'clock when I reached
the yourt.

The local men said there were good ibex near by,
so we decided to lie over a day. Next morning Kermit went with Rahima to look for ibex, and I went
back over the river to try to find the wounded buck.
We were able to pick up the trail, but after following
it for 400 yards through the thickest kind of jungle
we lost it. We quartered through the brush for a
couple of hours but could not find it.

Later in the morning we had a roe drive, mainly
to please Ishmael Bey, the "Big Beg." Personally,
I would rather still-hunt my game wherever it is
conceivably possible. Four men went whooping over
the hillside, while the Beg and I sat solemnly near

113

a rock where there was an open glade. All that went by was one doe, which I would not shoot, much to the grief of the Beg. Of course we intended to collect a doe for each group for the museum, but it seemed to us more fitting that in this case it should be "gentlemen first," and that ladies should follow only in the interests of science.

At noon Kermit and Rahima came back. They had seen nothing worth shooting, although they had found a number of ibex. There was a herd of thirty feeding on the mountain, just across the river from camp, but no good head. They had, however, come on a fairly fresh bear-track, which surprised us, as we had understood bears were very scarce.

The local shikaries were an interesting lot. Our men called them the "jungli wallahs," literally, "men of the woods," but a term generally used for a wild rough fellow. They were a little bit of everything—a native of Bokhara, a Kalmuk, and a Kazak. Perhaps the most unusual among them was the Bokharan. He was a tall, good-looking fellow, well built, and active. As far as we could gather he had come from Bokhara about eight years before, driven out as the result of some turn of the war. After wandering over much of central Asia, he had worked his way to these mountains and stopped. He had married a Kirghiz woman and was raising a hybrid family. Our means of communication were so limited that this was all we could gather. He re-

cited a number of names to us, such as Baku, Samar-
kand, and Tashkent, evidently to show he was a
travelled man of the world. He wore a wadded coat
and long voluminous trousers. My shorts amused
him. At the halts he would sometimes pat my bare
knees, shake his head, and smile. The Kalmuk was
thick-set, dark, and wore a pigtail. He was indefatigable. The Kazak was chunky, short, and rather
light-colored. He was a jovial little fellow, always
grinning. He looked like a jolly goblin. They were
all tough as nails. They could climb all day over
the mountains, and come in at night to all intents
and purposes as fresh as when they went out. As
far as mountain work was concerned, they were
hardier than the men we had brought from Kashmir. They also had eyes which were crosses between a telescope and a microscope. They would
pick up game when it was difficult for me to see it
even with field-glasses. Their real fault was that
they knew nothing of stalking, and tended to feel
that the way to approach game was to charge it.

In the afternoon I went out again with Khalil and
the Kazak. We went down the stream, crossed a
ford, and lay down in the grass on top of a high
shoulder. From there we watched the woods and
hills on either hand. We had been there about an
hour when the Kazak saw some roe browsing up a
little valley. We started toward them, but the wind
had shifted, and when we reached a ridge and looked

115

down we saw that they had scented us. There were five does and a buck. The buck was disappearing over a ridge out of range. The does scattered and went off in all directions. There was no use trying to follow, so we threaded our way quietly through the woods. We found many more does. Once we saw seven with one little buck. We also heard a buck calling. I was surprised at this, for I did not realize their calling season began so early. Finally, "over the last ridge," the Kazak pointed to a brown spot on the other side of the valley and said it was a good buck. It was too late to stalk, so I decided to try a long shot. Luck was with me. Over he tumbled and rolled down the slope. We scrambled down and found he was a nice six-pointer with fourteen and a half inch horns. After we tied him behind the saddle on the Kazak's horse, we rode back to camp, well satisfied by the afternoon's work.

Next day we had broken camp and the caravan was ready to march, when Rahima came up to say he had just seen a herd of ibex in which there were a number of really good heads. There was no question of what to do. We ordered the caravan to unload and started at once for the place where he had seen the game. We went as far as we could on horseback, and that was much farther than we could have gone on any plains-bred ponies. Finally it got too steep even for our mountain-ponies. By this time the ibex had crossed a ridge and lain down to rest

through the heat of the day. We took the second
nullah down-wind from them, and crawled up it.
When we got on a level with the animals, we crossed
into the nullah next to them, and very carefully
climbed up the rocks to where we could look into
the next ravine. There they were, about 150 to 200
yards away, lying strung out like a row of brown
stones down a stream-bed. Some were resting their
heads on the grass, more were looking around. There
were sixteen animals, and four of them, according to
Rahima, had horns better than fifty inches in length.
Kermit had won the first shot by our old-established
method of flipping a coin. He selected an old black
male and fired. I followed suit at another. In an
instant they were up and away, but not before we
had had a chance for more shots. We had shot badly,
for none of the animals fell. We were confident,
however, that we had not missed, and we followed
to the point where they had crossed the first ridge.
There two blood-trails up the mountain showed
where two of them had gone. Here we separated,
Kermit and Rahima going to the left in the direction taken by the first animal at which Kermit had
shot. Khalil, the "jungli wallah," and I followed the
blood-trails. They led straight up the mountain,
and when I say straight I am not speaking meta-
phorically, but literally. The climb seemed all but
perpendicular. After an hour's hard work Khalil suggested, ostensibly in my interest, that we give my

gun to the "jungli-wallah," and tell him to get the wounded animals while we went to camp ourselves. My pride would not permit this except as a last resort, so on we went. Shortly the two trails split. We held to the clearest and climbed on. If I had been told beforehand that I could have crossed some of the places I did, I would not have believed it. Soon it was "every man for himself and the devil take the hindmost." Khalil and the "jungli wallah" treated me as if I were one of themselves, and paid no attention to me at all. We climbed along the edges of precipices "with a drop into nothing below us as straight as a beggar can spit." We climbed up shoulders where every other rock was rotten and crumbled under our weight. Across gullies where rivers of slide rock lay we ran in order that we might not be caught in the avalanches we knew we would start. Once I very nearly was. I got out by going with the avalanche and working to one side where a firm rock jutted out, upon which I jumped. We got above the snow-line and plodded across drift after drift. High on the mountain we found the ram-chukor, birds something like the capercaillie. They had a very musical whistle and seemed quite tame. I suppose they had never seen people before. Three times that blood-trail crossed the top of the mountain. For five hours we followed it. Then it began to grow fainter and fainter, and finally pinched out. We were sure the animal was close, so we quartered

around, but without success. By this time it had
begun to snow and was getting late, so there was
nothing for it but to start to make our way back.
Climbing up a bad place may be difficult, but, as all
mountain-climbers will bear me witness, it is nothing to climbing down that same place. We had good
hard work getting down, and finally ended up on a
glacier. We scrambled to the foot and were more
than glad to see the horses below us. The telescopic
eyes of the man who led them had served us well.
He had seen us and had brought them around some
five miles to meet us. It was now nearly seven and
we were famished. With the exception of a cake of
chocolate which I had had, and which I had divided
among the three of us, we had eaten nothing since
a six-thirty breakfast. The pony man had brought
some cold mutton and bread, which we wolfed down.
While we were doing it the "jungli-wallah" spotted
some roe and immediately suggested that we go after
them. He then proceeded to map out a plan of campaign for us which gave him two fords of the river
and two hills to climb. While he was talking the
deer vanished in the dusk. It showed, though, what
a tough man he was to want to take on such work
in a sleet-storm at dusk, after the day we had had.

We got back to camp in the pitch-dark. I found
that Kermit and Rahima had not come in, so I sent
out men with lanterns to help them. Finally, about
nine I got worried, fearing that something had gone

wrong with Kermit's bad knee, and was about to start out to look myself when I heard them coming down the trail. They had had much the same day as I, with the notable exception that they had found their wounded animal, a fine fifty-two-inch head. They also saw another of the ibex just at dusk. On the way back Kermit had shot a fine buck roe. They had carried the ibex skin and horns for a long way, and were both glad of camp and hot food.

Our hard work on the trail of my wounded ibex was not waste effort, however. The "jungli-wallah," who had been with me, found him stone-dead a short distance from where we lost the trail. He was a splendid big fellow, his horns measuring fifty-five and a half inches. The other wounded animal was also found dead, close to the same place. He was not so large, but still was a good head, the horns measuring forty-seven inches.

On August 4 we resumed our march down the valley. The stream scolded over the rocks at our feet. The hills on either side were wooded, save where they thrust great rocky shoulders like buttresses through the forests. For one long stretch the trees on the left bank had been killed by fire. Their tall, bare skeletons, black and disconsolate, gave a sombre note to the landscape. In the late afternoon we came to a place where the stream bent sharply to the right, and almost without warning the Tekkes Valley lay before us. Behind us and on either hand lay tne tree-clad hills set off by the snow-capped mountains. In front lay the plain, an unbroken stretch of shimmering grass. Beyond it again were the mountains.

A few miles more brought us to Shutta. The town consists of a few rather well-built log cabins and some barracks where a detachment of Chinese troops are stationed. We had the usual yourt waiting for us. After we were settled, the General called on us. He is a "general," although I suppose his total command does not exceed twenty men. The poor fellow had a bad wound in his back. It looked like a stab from a knife, but as he did not volunteer any information, we felt that good manners would not permit any questions. We looked him over and did what we could for him, but I am afraid another winter will see him gazetted to another world.

Even though he was in real pain, he was as curious as a child, and, sitting beside me on the rug, he would lean over and feel the hobnails in my boots, or gaze with rapt attention at my tobacco-pouch when I filled my pipe. Curiosity is one of the principal characteristics of the people in this part of the world. The traveller soon gets used to rows of solemn faces gazing at him with as absorbed interest as if he were an animal in the zoo.

We spent but one night at Shutta. Across the Tekkes plain our guard consisted of four mounted soldiers. They were the first real "soldier men" we

121

had seen. They were better mounted and better
equipped than those of the plains of Turkestan.
Above all, they had the swagger that is so indispen-
sable to a good soldier. These soldiers were a mixed
lot racially. Some were Chinese, some evidently
Kalmuks, and some of racial blends it was impossible to guess. One in particular, a captain at Shutta,
was lean and tall with an aquiline nose, high cheek-
bones, and straight black hair that hung half-way
to his shoulders. If he had been in the United States,
he would have been classed unhesitatingly as an Indian.

The population of the Tekkes Valley is scant. It
can be divided roughly into four groups—Kalmuks,
Kirghiz, Kazaks, and strays and mixtures. The
Kalmuks are not very numerous. There is only one
small settlement at a town called Azak-Karaul.
We were told they did not number more than a few
hundred. Their dress is much the same as the others
—fur cap, long coat caught in at the waist with a
scarf, and high boots—but they wear pigtails, and no
other natives do. They are Buddhists, but, contrary
to the tenets of their religion, are great hunters and
real fighting men. The day after we left Shutta we
were accompanied by one little Kalmak not more
than fifteen years old, who rode like a centaur. At
the town where we stopped that night we did not
get a very friendly reception. The Kirghiz head-
man, not wishing to be held to account, tried to

escape to the woods. The little Kalmuk galloped after him and brought him back like a diminutive David leading in a Goliath.

The Kirghiz and Kazaks are more numerous and scattered over the valley. They tend to be less nomadic than the Kalmuks. In their villages there are frequent log cabins. They cultivate small patches of ground on the plain. Both are Mohammedans. They are, on the whole, rather timid.

As for the last group, it consists of a few Chinese in or attached to the army, men like the Bokharan and cross-breeds of all kinds. In this group come some very interesting people whom we met our first night out from Shutta at a village called Agyas. They were Russians. We noticed them first when we saw, in the group that gathered when we got to the village, a man as blond as a Swede. There were four men, three women, and their families. They came from just north of the Black Sea. As far as we could gather, for we spoke no common language, they were driven out during the war. They had put up neat little houses and were a part of the community. They were not slipping into the shiftless ways of the local tribesmen, but were adapting the wilderness to their needs like a "Swiss Family Robinson." They gave us the best bread we had had since we left the Residency in Srinagar. They were weaving cloth. They had a milk-separator. They had a sled, the first we had seen. Above all, they had a numerous family of delightful children, blue-eyed and fat as butter-balls. It made us very homesick for our own children, particularly as one very beguiling baby was just about the age of Kermit's youngest. We wanted to help them, but we had little or nothing to give until we found that they were anxious for medicine, when we gladly shared our rather scant store with them. It would be very interesting to be able to look ahead three generations and see what effect they have on the community. Perhaps they are the pioneers of an immigration, for the Tekkes is "white man's country." Perhaps they will be absorbed like a few drops of rain on a parched desert, and all that will remain will be some blue-eyed Kalmuks.

We made good time over the Tekkes plain, for we travelled at the cowboy jog, which "eats up the long miles like fire." The plain itself, during the first couple of days' travel, was not unlike many of our Western prairies over which I have ridden. It was covered with grass which would have supported great numbers of cattle. It seemed about ten or fifteen miles broad where we started and gradually spread out as we travelled down the valley. By the time we reached the Kooksu, it had changed to rolling ridges, which in turn gave place to steeper hills near the Kargaitash. Through its length it was cut by streams running north to the Tekkes River. Especially toward the Kargaitash these had worn picturesque and rugged canyons down which the water poured with a musical tumult. In the canyons were fir-trees which were not visible until the edge was reached. They formed such a sharp contrast with the treeless prairie that we felt as if a small bit of another country had been cut out and planted there. The main river looped and twined down the centre of the valley.

On the plain there were not many different species of birds, but certain types were plentiful. There were quite a number of larks and sparrows and a great many hawks. The hawks were of three kinds: a large bird, a medium bird, and a small bird, like the three bears of the story. They varied in frequency in inverse ratio to their size. The small hawks followed our marching column every day, like gulls in the wake of a ship, waiting for the larks and sparrows we flushed. The small birds seemed to know exactly what was going on, for they lay close and flew only a short distance before diving into the grass again. Some would lie so close that the horses nearly stepped on them. One little brown fellow refused to fly at all, and Kermit had to rein up his horse to let him scamper out of the way. The hawks were very graceful. They swept in great curves over the caravan. When they stooped they did so swifter than thought but with no apparent effort. Their swing was not interrupted when they struck their prey. There would be a few feathers floating in the

125

air, and the hawk sailing many yards away with the little bird in its talons. Along the line of march we flushed coveys of partridges which whirred up and away. Occasionally we found quail. Once a female pheasant rose ponderously and rumbled off.

As we crossed one stream, a very little one, we saw lots of small fish darting about. We stopped and fished in the oldest and most primitive fashion. Where the stream split, we dammed one channel at both ends. When the water had largely run out, we splashed among the stones and caught the fish in our hands. The largest was about four inches long. We got a couple of pounds. There were two kinds. One was like our catfish, with a rather broad mouth and barbels, but much thinner and longer in proportion. The other was also a slender fish, silver-sided with black dots, but with a fleshy, underhung, bottom-feeding mouth. They came in very handy, for that evening the pack-animals took the wrong trail and did not get in until nearly midnight. Those little fish were our supper, and very good they were too.

All across the valley we saw tumuli. They were low grass-covered mounds often arranged in a row. In a couple of places spring freshets had torn some to pieces and laid bare the rough stones of which they were built. They were evidently very old, for no one we met knew what they were or who had made them. For all we knew they might have looked on the armies of Ghenghiz Khan swirling down from the north to conquer the Eastern world.

On August 12 we reached Chin Ballak. It was a lovely evening. During the day it had rained, but as we made camp it cleared. The sun set banked in clouds of delicate pink and pearly gray. The mist-mantles gradually rolled up the mountains, leaving bare the rocky snow-ribbed peaks. The sky changed to a dull green, the light faded. Kermit and I sat in our roorkee chairs and smoked. We were content, for we had at last reached the heart of the hunting country of the Tian Shan.

CHAPTER VI

IN THE HEART OF THE HUNTING COUNTRY.
IBEX, SHEEP, AND BEAR

OUR knowledge of the geography of the Tian Shan range was very hazy. We had been unable to get any good maps, and what we could gather from the Kazaks and Kalmuks through the medium of our shikaries, only further confused us. Kargaitash had always been our goal for hunting ovis karelenyi, but whether it was a nullah or a mountain we could never make sure. The small-scale maps which we possessed showed it as a somewhat indefinite range of mountains; but from our questionings we gathered that that was not what the Kazaks meant when referring to Kargaitash.

After leaving our camp in the Kooksu we headed gradually into the hills, through pine forests where we were told the wapiti lived, and over one or two small passes. On the crest of these barren passes, amid the rocks and snow, wild flowers ran riot—yellow and purple pansies, dainty primula, and many whose names we could not approximate. It was hard to say where they were most effective—in the glades of the pine forests or among the lonely rocks. Rahima summed up the situation in laconic fashion when he remarked: "Here jungle all same as garden."

128

Ever since crossing the Muzart we had been doing our best to get in touch with one or another of the natives, Kazak or Kalmuk, with whom Rahima had hunted on his previous expeditions in the Tian Shan. He had been here twelve years ago, and as far as we could learn there had been no sahibs in the country since then; first there was the war, and afterward the approach through Russia was closed. Of his two Kalmuk friends, Namgoon had died and Nurla was away, but eventually there turned up one Tula Bai, a Kazak, of whom Rahima thought very highly. He was a short man and walked doubled over, giving a gorilla-like appearance. The first few days he was our guide, his mind, to put it kindly, seemed elsewhere, for we doubled about every which way, much to the disgust of our head pony man, who did not hesitate to explain to Tula Bai with some warmth the error of his ways. Ted and I reserved judgment, which was about all we could do; but when once we got straightened out and really in the hunting country, we found that Rahima had not overrated the old fellow.

We stopped at a number of Kazak khourgas to bargain for horses, for we wished to spell our riding-ponies when we started in hunting. We also had sheep to buy for food for ourselves and the men. In one khourga we found a large hooded eagle. Its owner told us that he used it for coursing roe-deer and also for wapiti; but in the latter case he can

129

only have meant partly grown wapiti. The eagle was not a silent bird; it called out incessantly, but the other occupants of the khourga paid no attention to it; there was a fat baby asleep in a cradle right beside the perch. At another halt we came on a young bull wapiti, perhaps eighteen months old and entirely friendly with his captors.

As we climbed, the weather became colder; the rain, which had been an almost daily occurrence, changed to snow and sleet on the passes, and one could imagine how bitter cold it must be in the winter months if this was what we found in midsummer. The wandering Kazaks had come far up the valleys with their horses and cattle and sheep to take advantage of the summer pasturage. The cattle in particular were fine big animals, but apparently they are rarely slaughtered for food. The chief use made of them seemed to be for riding. In these high pastures there is a poisonous grass to which the herds pay toll, and more than once we came upon dead sheep.

Unexpectedly one afternoon the riddle of Kargaitash was solved for us when Tula Bai pointed out a long, flat-topped butte crowned with tall, irregular pencils of black rock. This was Kargaitash, the stone trees, as the words signify in Turki. Near its base, at an altitude of slightly more than 9,000 feet, we pitched our camp. The cold rain and the mist-clad mountains made it evident that hunting could not be continuous.

Rahima was greatly disappointed when we found that several bands of Kalmuks had preceded us by ten or twelve days and were engaged in shooting marmots. They had old single-shot rifles of the model of 1876, and though they confined their attentions to the marmots, he was afraid that they would have disturbed the country and driven the sheep elsewhere. Kazak and Kalmuk are in continual feud, and it behooves the sahib to watch out that whichever is with him does not make use of the shadow of his wing to oppress the enemy. Our Kazaks did their utmost to persuade us to allow them to confiscate the rifles and ponies of the Kalmuks on the plea that they had disturbed our hunting country.

On August 15 Ted and I set out in opposite directions from camp. Khalil and Tula Bai were with me, while Ted had Rahima and a shenzi named Nurpay, the possessor of a remarkable pair of eyes. Our Kazaks wore hide breeches, and many a ride in the rain had bagged them abnormally at the knees. They reminded us of Father's story of how on the station platform at Medora, North Dakota, a slightly intoxicated stranger walked round and round his ranch foreman eying his leather trousers, and finally broke out with: 'Well, if you're going to jump, jump, damn you!'"

We rode cautiously along, dismounting below the crest of each hill and crawling to the top, field-glasses in hand, to spy out the country. The first wild animal to be sighted was a marmot sitting at the mouth of its burrow. These dark-skinned little fellows are much sought after by the Kalmuks, and we were told that at Kulja a good hide would bring three dollars. At Ayalik, when after ibex, I saw three of them tumbling about in the grass. One adult female I measured was thirty inches over all.

The next game we caught sight of from a subsequent rise was a roe-deer. Tula Bai informed me that it was a tika-illik—an ibex-roe—that its mother had been an ibex and its father a roe; but as a careful examination failed to show us any signs of this unusual mésalliance in the offspring, we decided to leave it alone for fear of disturbing any Karelini that might be within hearing.

Not long after this Khalil made out a small ram climbing up a steep hill. When it had topped the crest, we hurried after it. There were a great many crows on the hillside wheeling and clustering most agitatedly. It was evident that there were some disturbers of the peace in the offing. As we got nearer, we found that a brown hawk, lighter in body than any crow, was endeavoring to make a kill. He invariably attacked the crows upon the ground; six times I saw him swoop unsuccessfully. Half a dozen crows followed in his wake, attempting to mob him, but he paid little attention to them, avoiding them with the greatest of ease whenever they seemed to be uncomfortably close. Our way led through the scene of the combat, so we dispersed the gathering.

At the brow of the hill Khalil and I had our field-glasses ready, and soon picked up three Karelini rams, feeding on a patch of grass a mile or more away. Our first stalk was a failure. Verily in this country "the wind bloweth where it listeth," and a sudden eddy made our quarry suspicious. They could have got only a very faint whiff, for they trotted off slowly while we watched them from behind a rocky ridge. We saw that in addition to the three marked down there had been as many more hidden. One was Khalil's small ram, and the others were clearly big fellows; Khalil and Tula Bai estimated them as all having horns more than fifty inches in length. Although they were between five and six hundred yards from us, Khalil was eager for me to open fire, insisting that I would get no second chance. His judgment of the proper time to shoot was very often faulty. Trotting across a narrow valley, they climbed a long, easy, sloping ridge. As they crossed a stretch of snow their horns stood clearly outlined, and we realized that those of the last one were larger than the others; but it was when he clambered upon a rock on the ridge crest and framed himself against the blue sky that we saw him in his full glory and appreciated his true size. Khalil turned to me: "If master get him, I give God twenty rupees at Bandipur!"

Tula Bai, although ready to go anywhere on horse-back, was not of much use on foot; in addition, he was inclined to be crotchety and opinionated, so I sent him back to the ponies. When the sheep passed out of sight, Khalil and I made all speed toward where we had last seen them. We found that they had stopped seven or eight hundred yards farther on; some were lying down, others were feeding. The only way to get within range involved a long détour, and included some stiff climbing. An hour's work, the most disagreeable part of which was the crossing of two wide and steeply inclined snow-fields where we started a couple of small avalanches and felt in a very precarious and uncomfortable position, brought us to a ridge running down near where the sheep lay. Now was the time to make haste slowly, for a misstep and a loosened boulder would give us away. All went well and at a short 150 yards I fired.

We had picked out the old ram; he was lying down facing away from me, and I made precisely the same shot as I had with my ibex at Khanayalik. A bullet entering from behind and ranging forward is almost inevitably fatal. Although he ran, I knew he could not go far, so I turned my attention to his companions. I wanted four sheep. They ran off quartering and then swung around, uncertain whence the trouble came. Part of the time they were hidden in a ravine. I did some rapid shooting, fifteen shots, and when we hurried down to take stock we found that I had bagged five instead of four; one had fallen in the ravine without my knowing it. Only the small one got away. Ted said that whenever we shot at a number of animals it was, according to our shikaries, invariably a case of "The boys with their rakes killed twenty-five snakes, but the biggest one got away!" This time I had made any such theory untenable.

Upon measuring the heads we found that, although the four smaller heads were not as large as we hoped, ranging from forty-four to forty-six inches, the large one was bigger than we had dared to think possible. Around the curve these horns taped sixty-one inches. More than an inch larger than any head yet recorded. There was a great difference in coloration in these sheep. Our shikaries and the natives had told us that the darkest sheep were the largest, but in this case the big one had the lightest coat; three of the others were dark, and one light-colored.

It was four o'clock by the time we began the measuring and the skinning. We made out three Kazak herdsmen in a valley two or three miles away. Tula Bai gathered them in and we were glad of their help. Rain and sleet set in; skinning was bitterly cold work; but eventually I had two entire skins and three head-skins ready, and we packed them all over to the ponies across some very broken ground. On the ride back to camp Tula Bai took the lion's share of the load. On his pony he piled the two whole skins, leg-bones and all, roping a head on each side of the saddle, and perching himself on top. It was quarter to seven, very dark and cold and wet, but he set out undaunted in the lead. In places the ground was boggy and the ponies sank and struggled; elsewhere there were only rocks and holes, and dimly discerned precipices, along the very edges of which we skirted, but through it all Tula Bai's white pony, "like the crested plume of the brave Navarre," glimmered in our van. A white pony is a conspicuous hunting companion, and in the morning I had looked upon it with a very disapproving eye, but at night my feelings were altogether reversed. Khalil sang in Kashmiri and I in English and somehow or other the long, cold hours passed until half past nine, when we caught the glimmer of our camp-fire, after fifteen hours' hunting.

Ted had had a most interesting time, for although he had seen no heads worth shooting, he had counted a great quantity of game—three herds of Karelini ewes and young, totalling thirty-five animals, and two herds of ibex, totalling eighty. It certainly seemed as if we were in a country teeming with game, but the promise was not fulfilled. We were at a loss to understand the subsequent scarcity; the best explanation we could contrive was that the Kalmuks, coming up from the valleys after marmot-skins, had driven the large game to distant and unknown feeding-grounds. Ted hunted long hours every day for the ensuing week without getting a shot at a sheep. He was usually off twelve to fourteen hours and scoured the country in every direction, while camp was shifted hither and yon as seemed most likely to put us in the sheep country.

Ted never saw another herd of ewes; twice he caught sight of rams, once of ten and once of four, but on neither occasion could he and Rahima get within range, although using every effort and the greatest caution in watching the treacherous air-currents.

Twice he came upon ibex, on each occasion getting three; out of the first lot the best head measured forty-six inches, out of the second the best was fifty-two. Ibex-hunting, unless you have the time and inclination to wait for ideal conditions, involves an immense amount of hard climbing with a distinct spice of danger thrown in. One day Ted took out a pair of rubber-soled shoes to try and they proved most unsatisfactory, almost costing him his life when he slipped and started rolling.

These long hunting-days were not attended by ideal weather. There was generally a potpourri of sunshine, rain, sleet, and snow, the various elements predominating upon different days. Fords, too, were obstacles, swelled by snow-water in the afternoon and evening, and on a certain night Ted and Rahima were nearly washed away. The only insect pest was a large fly, bigger than a horse-fly but with a sting not so severe—indeed, no worse than a mosquito. It was their multitude and their buzzing that caused most annoyance. Fortunately, they were late to rise and early to bed. When the sun was hidden they miraculously disappeared, but when the sun came out they equally miraculously reappeared. If you tried to use your field-glasses, they bustled about your face and neck and entangled themselves in your beard. Then you would call for clouds, but when the sun was darkened it became so cold that you felt ready again to undergo the fly pest.

Our battery consisted of two Springfields and two Hoffman .375's. Both were admirably suited to our work. The Hoffman is a beautifully turned out fire-arm, excellently balanced and sighted. One felt that with it there were no alibis available when one missed.

After getting the Karelini rams I turned my attention to collecting females to complete the various groups. I was fortunate enough to find a herd of about twenty ewes late one afternoon. There was a long plateau skirting a river with deep ravines running down to the valley. The sheep were moving along from one draw to another, feeding. A long but comparatively simple stalk brought me within easy range, and to our Karelini group was added its female.

The long day's hunting always showed something of interest. Twice I came upon foxes—big red fellows with white tips to their tails. The first was hunting field-mice, and was very graceful as he pounced upon his quarry. He was entirely unaware of us, and I could have had an easy shot but that I was afraid of frightening some particularly fine ibex that had been seen near by. Parenthetically, I never did find the ibex, but had I shot the fox I would undoubtedly have laid it to that; it was just one of those cases when you are wrong either way. The second fox I met was stalking a covey of fourteen ramchukor, the big mountain-grouse, larger than a pheasant; a marmot sitting at the entrance to his burrow was an interested spectator, playing the part of innocent bystander. This time I had no chance for a shot.

The hawks as well as the foxes must have lived largly upon mice. Their runways were everywhere; we collected two kinds, one larger than a common house-mouse and with a very short tail, the other only half the size but with a tail almost as long as its body. The former the men caught one night in camp, the latter I saw in the grass and captured by throwing myself off my pony on top of it. It was a good many years since I had prepared any small mammals, and Ted was vastly amused at the pride I took in the skins when I had them stuffed and pinned out, looking, I must own, very plethoric and misshapen.

We constantly felt the lack of a .410 shotgun. On the heights we saw numerous ramchukor, and on the grassy uplands many a covey of partridges. I shot one of the former with my Springfield. A .410 or a

.22 Winchester makes so little noise that there is, as a rule, no danger of disturbing the country.

I got a female ibex for the group after a long day among the canyons and ridges of Kargaitash. The columns of rock had been worn into every fantastic shape. Some were like sphinxes, others like strange birds and beasts. Often erosion had left a great rock perched precariously upon the top of a tall, slender column. Sometimes a solitary stem would arise like a great factory chimney. Ted described the whole scene, as he saw it lighted by the sunset, as reminding him of the sky-line of New York. I came upon some ibex lying on isolated rocky pedestals just as the chamois is always shown in the school geographies.

It is most difficult to judge at all correctly the length of the horns of any animal. A ram's horn with its convolutions is naturally more difficult to estimate than that of an ibex; but even the latter presents enough room for error. One evening when we were riding down a deep gulch, with a female Siberian roe for the group as the day's contribution, we saw a herd of ibex grazing on the mountains. An hour and a half's stalk would have been called for to put us in range, and by that time it would have been long after dark, so we contented ourselves with studying them through field-glasses and telescope. Khalil felt certain that there were no heads better than forty-five inches in length, but we nevertheless determined next day to go after them, for time was passing and we had the wapiti group still unstarted. We felt that it would be a very difficult one to get and would require as many days as we could manage to devote to it.

The following morning Ted set off with Rahima across the Kooksu in the hope of coming on ovis karelini, while Khalil and I went to look up these ibex. We had not been gone long when we got a glimpse of six wild pig bustling through the undergrowth on the opposite side of the ravine. Some hasty shots resulted mainly in misses, but the big boar turning back and away from the rest gave us the idea that he might be hit. The underbrush was chiefly made up of a dwarf juniper with wide and low trailing branches. The boar disappeared into a dense, isolated bit of jungle and, upon his failing to reappear, we started toward the clump in which we had last seen him. The mountainside was a maze of pig trails and up it we toiled; the going would have been easier had we been closer to the pig in stature. At length we reached the boar's retreat, to find ourselves in a warren of big burrows, down one of which our quarry had gone.

We were now well up the mountain, and decided to keep climbing and then make our way as best we could along the ridge, for it was on this side of the nullah that we had seen the ibex. A lammergeyer circled above us; Khalil remarked that that "big bird" always brought him luck; also he had dreamed propitiously during the night. All this was encouraging, but it didn't make our path any easier. Around rocky peaks, over runways of slide rock, among heaped-up broken boulders we scrambled and slid until we came to a vantage-point from which we could see the mountainside where we believed the ibex would go for their day's siesta. They were so much the color of the gray rocks that it was a long time before we could pick them out; but gradually we discovered one after another. An ibex sleeps in the most outlandish positions; here one was sprawled along the ledge with his head hanging down between two rocks; there one lay flat on his side on a sand slide so steep that he seemed through the glasses to be standing up; you would not find more postures in a barrack-room of sleeping soldiers. We were about 800 yards away, and examined their heads carefully. Khalil said that there was none with horns fifty inches in length, but I was inclined to disagree with him. The females lay between us and the big males in such a manner as to make stalking impossible until they moved, so there was nothing to do but wait.

We had become very hot in the course of our three and a half hours' climb, so of the two evils we rather preferred the flies and the sun to shivering in the fly-less cold. A marmot came out on a near-by peak and sat up chattering and wagging his tail like an automaton. Some ramchukor sailed whirring by, but the ibex showed no desire to move. It started to rain, then it sleeted, then it snowed. I went a little way down one side of the hill in order to walk up again and get warmed. At length the ibex got up; exasperatingly slowly, with false starts, hesitating and retracing their steps, they picked their way down-hill. Noting their direction, we made all haste to cut them off. We topped a ridge and saw them 250 yards away. If I had used better judgment I could have gotten a hundred yards closer, but it is hard for a shikarry to realize some of the difficulties of the sahib with the rifle; he may be winded, but he needs no steady hand; and seen with his keen eyes game looks close and a very satisfactory target. Khalil always wanted me to shoot at longer ranges than necessary. This time, however, I was committed; the ibex were suspicious and I must shoot. My first bullet took effect; my second misfired and lost me an excellent chance. There followed a fusillade as they dodged about among the rocks. Summed up, I had wounded two, one of which I finished with my last two cartridges. Even when he lay dead we didn't realize his size; I judged fifty inches, Khalil less, but the tape showed fifty-nine and a half. This made him the largest of recorded heads by an inch and three-quarters.

Darkness was rapidly approaching. Nurpay had heard us and followed up the valley. We got the skin off and down the mountainside. It was packed on Nurpay's pony, and how, hampered by the great sweep of the horns, he steered his way through the thickets and the boulders in the pitchy blackness, I failed to understand. Of course it was raining. Once more I was glad for a white hunting-pony, as I prodded my old horse along just managing to keep in sight. At half past eight we reached our most welcome camp-fire. Ted was not yet in, but at nine he rode up, drenched but cheerful with a fifty-two-inch ibex. He had been all but washed away in fording the river, and we had a busy time drying his kodak first and then his other belongings that required less urgent attention.

Next day camp was moved in the direction of the Kensu country. It was not to be a long march, so Khalil, Nurpay, and I went off after the wounded ibex. We were convinced that he had not gone far, but by the time we had reached the mountain crest where we had last seen him lying down, snow and hail came pelting down, washing away all tracks, and the mist billowed up the ravines, closing in on every side. A rumbling of avalanches and some dimly seen skipping boulders bound toward where we had left our ponies did not add to our comfort. After a few hopeless casts we felt forced to abandon the search, and very wet and bedraggled we finally reached our new camping-grounds late in the afternoon.

Another short march planted us on the banks of the Kensu in what was to be a five days' hunting-camp. A lovely valley closed in by high mountains, pines on the lower slopes, then junipers and low bushes, above them the débris of landslides, broken barren boulders, with an occasional flower in the crevices, and, crowning all, the eternal snows. Edelweiss grew in profusion, and many other flowers were familiar Alpine friends.

From here we had ibex, mountain-sheep, and wapiti shooting all within reach, but it was pre-eminently ibex ground. Nomenclature of game has always interested me. Father was keen on preserving native names wherever possible, but pioneers and settlers are apt to call an animal after the beast it most nearly resembles back in their homeland. Sometimes the similarity is far from close, as with the mighty rapier-horned antelope that the Boers christened the gemsbuck.

An *onomatopoetic* name always pleased Father, such as quagga for zebra in imitation of the animal's barking cough, or bwehar for jackal, copying its howl. Father did not at all approve of the American wapiti being called an elk after the Norwegian moose, and there can be no question but that his hunting-books have had a great deal to do with fastening the native Indian name upon that handsomest of the existing deer family.

It would have both interested and amused Father to find our native American name bestowed upon the wapiti's Asiatic cousin. Our Kashmiri shikaries, getting the name from British sportsmen, referred to the big deer as wapiti. The general native name was boogha, a slight variation, if any, of the name for Yarkand stag. Our Kashmiris called ibex "ibuckus," and it was as that we usually referred to them. Their native name in the Tian Shan is "tikka." Siberian roe is known as "illik," and when Rahima first talked of it we believed that he was Kashmirizing elk and was speaking about the wapiti.

Accompanying us we had a small flock of fat-tailed sheep, whose number was decimated to fill the needs of ourselves and our followers. The mutton was excellent, very different from the stringy stuff with which we had wrestled on the trek across the plains of Turkestan. A most agreeable addition to our larder were the mushrooms that abounded in the valley. Ted measured one that was twelve inches in diameter, but the little button fellows were the better eating. There were two kinds; one pinkish beneath and seemingly identical with our home mushroom we greatly preferred to a larger sort, white underneath, tasting not unlike the fungus beloved of Italians.

With a lucky shot from the Springfield I knocked over a ramchukor, but Rousslia was not much of a hand at preparing game, and the big bird was not the success we had hoped. At all events I prepared his skin, so we did not feel he was lost.

Each day brought its individual interest, a glimpse of some new mammal or bird, a difficult ford to cross or crag to scale. We needed another ibex for the group, and one day when Khalil was feeling crocked up and needed a rest in camp, I took Nurpay with me and started off for the ibex grounds.

As we were climbing up the mountain I twice saw ferrets, little brown-and-white fellows, far too spry for us to catch, although we did our best. They lived in burrows among the rocks. Farther on we came upon several places which wolves had been using as open-air dens. There must have been a good-sized pack, for between the boulders we traced many hollows where they had bedded down. They had been killing ibex and had dragged their quarry some distance down the mountain, for we were still way beneath the ibex country. Of the ibex heads scattered about the rocks, none were of more than thirty inches in length. I only once heard wolves. It was early one frosty morning when the lower hills were covered with a light snowfall. The wolves were in full cry, a musical though sinister sound, with occasional breaks that reminded me of a chorus of hyenas with their insane laughter.

We did a lot of climbing before we sighted ibex, but we were well above them and could study them at our leisure. I made up my mind that there was no head much better than forty-five inches in length, but there were several with fine, massive horns. Selecting the handsomest for my target, I let drive. He went off almost as if unhit, but Nurpay was not to be deceived and said that I had got him. Cau-

147

tiously we clambered down and found our ibex hanging by one horn from a narrow ledge of rock. Beneath was a sheer drop of 500 feet. The horn was jammed so hard into a crevice that it took our united strength to free it. It had, however, not only saved us a long and most difficult climb down and back, but almost certainly the fall into the canyon would have hopelessly smashed the ibex, rendering both hide and head useless to the museum. We found it no slight task to skin the animal in the little niche into which we dragged it. One slip nearly cost Nurpay his life.

The morning after we reached our Kensu camp Ted took the side of the valley on which our tent was pitched, while I crossed over and started up the mountains opposite, accompanied by Khalil and Nurpay. We had been climbing for about an hour and a half when we came upon a marmot burrow scored with the claws of a bear. He had slipped in his attempt to catch the little rodent, and it was clear that the tracks were of the night before. Hitherto we had seen a great deal of bear sign, but nothing more recent than three or four days old. Here was a chance for the dogs, so I sent Nurpay back to camp for them while Khalil and I climbed on up the mountain, partly to look for game and partly with the idea that we would be above the dogs, and able to watch their line and get to them quicker in case they came to terms with the bear.

While we were watching a herd of ibex—there were

no good heads among them—I thought I heard the dogs give tongue. Khalil was sure I hadn't, so we continued to rake the country with our field-glasses until the time we had allotted for Nurpay's return was almost up. We hurried back to the vantage-point whence the marmot hole was visible; there were Nurpay's and Fezildin's ponies, but neither riders nor hounds to be seen. I had told Nurpay to put the dogs on the trail and loose them. We called out but there was no answer; we felt sure the hunt had gone away without us, but we had commanded one possible direction while watching the ibex, so off we boiled in the opposite, heeding little for falls. My bad knee was thrown out but not seriously. Every little while we stopped to listen for the hounds, and each ridge we topped we hoped to catch sight of the chase; but ridge succeeded ridge and nothing could be seen. Disconsolately we returned to the ponies. We reached them exasperated and breathless at quarter past one, to find men and dogs asleep in the grass. Through a misunderstanding the dogs had not been loosed and the men had not heard our hallooing.

The trail was now far too stale to follow, for there had been a scorching sun all morning, so after a very brief tiffin, I sent Fezildin and the dogs back to camp, and plodded once more up the mountain. We had moved from one ridge to another when, at four o'clock, Khalil announced that he saw a bear. Nurpay brought the telescope to focus on it, and at first insisted that it was a tungus, a pig; but it only took a good look for me to feel sure he was mistaken. It was a bear right enough, walking up a grassy nullah far off on the opposite side of the mountain from that up which we had climbed. There was a long stalk before us, and no time to lose. We slithered and slipped down the bed of a ravine which was floored with slide rock. It was almost as much work as climbing. We had started from Srinagar outfitted with beautiful steel-shod khud sticks, but they had all but one succumbed to the vicissitudes of mountain-trekking, and the one remaining was sadly cracked and weakened. We usually trusted to picking up a makeshift stick, but to-day I had none, and badly did I miss it. There were two steep hillsides up which to pant and struggle before we reached the nullah in which we had seen the bear. Cautiously we pushed ourselves through the dwarf junipers. We could see nothing, and separated to different vantage-points. I kept a sharp eye on the other two, and soon saw Khalil signalling. On reaching him he pointed out the bear, lying curled up in the undergrowth a hundred and fifty yards away, on the other slope of the nullah. As I fired, it jumped up and rolled over and over into the bed of the ravine, shouting and howling. Khalil said it was finished, but wishing to make certain, I fired a couple of shots at the rolling bear but scored no hit. We launched ourselves down into the nullah, though

Nurpay kept exclaiming that there was no way down and we would all fall. In safety we landed, but the bear was gone. We caught a fleeting glimpse of something running through the underbrush and once more I opened fire. Nurpay turned cautious; he was manifestly a great respecter of bears, but he was too loyal not to follow in our wake. Two hundred yards down the ravine we stopped to reconnoitre, and then it was that Nurpay caught sight of a bear's ears well up the side down which we had come. He had some difficulty in making Khalil and me see it, but at last I did. With the second shot, down came the bear, shot through the heart, bounding from rock to rock, to bring up stone-dead within thirty yards of us.

It was an old he-bear, very fat. We had no time for taking stock and congratulating ourselves, for it was after six. I hastily jotted down the measurements, tried a time exposure with my kodak, and we settled down to the skinning with desperate earnest. Daylight was about gone when we started back up the ravine, but of a sudden Nurpay stopped; his keen eyes had picked up a blood-trail. "Yekke aya," "two bears," he said. Khalil stoutly maintained that there had been but one; I sided with Nurpay, for a number of details, hitherto unnoticed, came back to me. First there was the color; the original bear had seemed almost white, while the one we were carrying was dark brown. Then thinking back over the hasty skinning, I could but recall one bullet-hole. Last of all, I was sure that the bear could not have been down in the nullah here and have climbed so far when I shot him. Still, for the night it was purely an academic discussion; it was far too late to hope to follow a trail.

We turned our attention to the serious work of getting ourselves and the bearskin back to camp. First Nurpay and I tried to carry it tandem, but one would slip and drag down the other, and but little headway was made. On a perpendicular hill slope we halted and I skinned out the head, mainly by feel. The head with the flesh on it must have weighed twenty pounds. I hung it like a pendant round my neck. With our mufflers we slung the skin about Nurpay, and once more got under way. A quarter-moon appeared, but in half an hour it was hidden by clouds. We struggled along with frequent halts. Part of the time we walked upright, except for frequent falls among the rocks; up the steeper bits we crawled on hands and knees. There was no chance to pick our path; we got over or round whatever appeared in front of us. It was after eleven before we won our way back to the ponies, but fortunately the threatening rain had held off until we were mounted. Still once more I had cause to see the advantages of a white hunting-pony. Nurpay on his white mare threaded his way down the mountain-side as only a Kazak can, over country that might

THE RECORD KARELINI

NURPAY AND THE BEAR

well give pause in daylight. The ponies seemed by instinct to avoid the marmot holes, and when they did step into one, they showed the utmost calmness in extricating themselves. When we came upon small patches of upland meadow, there were always hidden springs and the ground was boggy; by night we could only trust to Nurpay's instinct and our ponies' experience. I had a long inward debate as to whether, if I groped around for pipe, tobacco, and matches, the discomfort of lighting my pipe would be compensated for in the subsequent comfort of a smoke. I made the effort and was rewarded, although my pony all but came down when I loosened the reins to strike a match. At half past twelve we rode into camp, and tumbled from our saddles to thaw ourselves round a blazing fire of spruce logs, and recount our adventures to the sleepy men who had rolled out of their blankets when they heard us coming.

In the morning Khalil was feeling too done up to go out, so I took two Kazaks and went off to look into the matter of the possible second bear. Nurpay had been right; there had been two, and we followed the one I had first wounded for three-quarters of a mile down the ravine below where the other had fallen. The trail was most difficult, and at length it was lost, even to Kasin's sharp eyes. We made futile casts in every direction, but at last we had to abandon the chase. I had debated taking the dogs, and it would have been well had I done so, but in the first place the existence of a second bear was doubtful, and in the second I was afraid that a badly wounded bear might so cut up our dogs as to destroy their further usefulness.

A few days later we both took the dogs out, thinking that if the wounded bear were still alive we might pick up its fresh trail. Either it or another had been working about in the nullah bottom, for Lead immediately showed interest. He and Rollie puzzled a trail out for a short distance, but it was evidently too stale to follow through to a successful conclusion.

CHAPTER VII

THE ASIATIC WAPITI OF THE TIAN SHAN

"And they travelled far, and further than far."
—OLD FAIRY STORY.

THERE are many ibex in the Tian Shan mountains, but any one who believes that a good head is therefore easy to get makes a very real mistake. It is one thing to see them through the field-glasses, and another to get them and bring them back in triumph to camp. Stalking the big ibex is hard and tricky work.

The day after we reached the Ken River, Rahima Loon and I started out for our tenth day of fruitless search for the Karelini. "Here and there like a dog at a fair" we wandered over rolling, turf-covered hills. Whenever we drew near a place from which we could get a wide view of the country beyond, we dismounted and crawled to the crest like little boys playing Indian. It was almost dark and we had worked up into the rocky mountains before we saw anything. Then it was not Karelini but a large flock of ibex. At first there seemed to be nothing but females, kids, and young males. I counted sixty-four, and there may have been more, for some, like the little pigs in the story, skipped around so fast I could

155

not count them accurately. We watched them as they wandered down through the rocks to browse in the grassy nullahs. At times the young males would spar and butt one another, for all the world like their domestic cousins the goats. They were thoroughly alert, nevertheless, and the advance-guard of the troop as they stepped daintily along would pause every few minutes, look carefully in all directions, and snuff the air. Suddenly Rahima Loon nudged me and whispered: "Burra wallah!" (big fellow). They were lying around a large rock. Some could be seen entirely. Others were half hidden by the rock. At times they would get up, stretch, and look around. At times they would lie on their sides with their horns resting on the ground. There was no doubt that they were big, for the horns showed the sweeping curve that comes only with age and size.

There was no chance to stalk them. Long before we could have reached their rocky stronghold, it would have been too dark to shoot. We watched until the light failed, and planned our campaign for the next day.

Early next morning we left camp. For seven long hours we toiled over ridges and, like the wizards, "peeped and muttered," for the ibex had shifted their ground during the night and we could not find them. It was afternoon when we finally sighted them again. The big males were lying high on the hillside with the rest of the flock spread fan-wise around them. Two stalks lay open to us: one over the top of the mountain, the other up a nullah to a point where the small fry that surrounded the big animals were fewest. We chose the latter, as it was shorter, and for nearly three hours we worked our way toward them. The last half-mile was over slide rock. Trying to walk over slide rock without noise is like trying to cross a room in the dark without up-setting a chair. Careful as we were, an occasional rock would clatter down the slope. Before we got within range the noise alarmed the females, and the whole herd began moving away over a ridge. We made a desperate eleventh-hour attempt to cut them off but failed, and rode disconsolately into camp in the dark.

By this time, however, I was reasonably sure that I knew the general habits of these particular ibex. Next day Kermit and I decided to hunt them to-gether. We started with our shikaries and "jungli wallahs" about five next morning. A thick hoar-frost covered the grass. It was nipping cold. The ponies shivered as they stood hunched up under the saddles. As we rode up the nullah that led to the hunting-grounds the sun had reached the mountain crests, painting their snow-caps a delicate rose pink. By contrast the dark cold valley where we were seemed even darker and colder.

We rode up the side of a ridge that would in many circles be considered very fair mountaineering on foot, for a Kazak pony climbs as if it had a monkey in its ancestry. Just below the crest we dismounted and tied our horses. Then we got out our field-glasses and searched the mountainside. In a short time we found the flock, tiny light-brown specks on the slate-gray rock. A few minutes later we spotted our big fellows. They were in the same relative position they had held on the two previous days, in the rocks two or three hundred yards below the snow-line, with the rest of the herd in a crescent around them. After a hurried discussion, we decided that the best approach was to work up the reverse slope of the shoulder on which we were to the crest of the mountain, then to push our way through the snow until we were directly above them. Accordingly, we set out for a preliminary four miles of what Kermit calls "side-hill grouging," that is, walking diagonally across the face of a slope with an angle of forty-five degrees. There are different kinds of grouging. There is, for example, walking along the side of a partially turf-covered hill. This is not bad. Then there is walking along a slide-rock slope where it is possible to diagonal in two directions. This is harder, for there is always the danger of starting a rock-slide. Last and worst is grouging a slide-rock slope for a long distance in the same direction. Here there is not only the danger of a landslip but, in addition, the up-hill side of the feet become very sore. On this stalk the first four miles were on the right sides of our feet and mainly over slide rock.

As we walked along the west slope of the ridge, three great ramchukor zoomed over us from the opposite side. Kermit and I both started, for they sounded exactly like seventy-seven shells. I believe if there had been a shell-hole handy, we would have instinctively run to it.

After two hours' climbing we reached the snow, and through it we ploughed for another mile to a point we had marked as nearest the animals. We worked cautiously over a jutting rock and saw the big ibex below us. They were nearly 300 yards away, and were half concealed by the overhang of the rock around which they were lying. A hasty whispered conference ensued. We decided to go on through the snow until we were on the other side of them, and then work down a rocky buttress to a point from which they would be about one hundred yards distant. Going through the snow it was reasonably easy to be quiet, but when we got to the rocks it was very different. We were so close that any noise might alarm the game. We watched every step and tested the footholds before putting weight on it. The wind was treacherous and gusty, as it generally is in the mountains, and this was an additional source of worry. Fortune was with us, however, and we got to the spot we had picked without frightening the ibex. After cautiously looking them over, we prepared to shoot. At this critical moment one of our shikaries lost his head and ran like a wild man along the sky-line. The game saw him and were alarmed. There was no time to be lost. It was my first shot and I fired just as they were moving off. Kermit followed suit immediately. We wounded but did not stop our animals. In a moment we caught sight of them again as they ran swiftly in single file through the rocks somewhat farther away. Again we fired in the same order. Luck perched on our shoulders, for both ibex fell and rolled head over heels down the steep slope. My animal was dead but Kermit's, though very groggy, was up and away again. Kermit finally stopped him with a phenomenally long shot near the mountain crest. We started for our kills at once. Rahima and a Kazak went with me, Khalil and another Kazak with Kermit. My buck had rolled some three or four hundred yards down-hill. It is surprising how far animals will roll down these steep mountainsides, sometimes with disastrous re-sults to their horns. Several times I have nearly rolled down a mountain with an ibex while trying to skin him where he had fallen.

When we got to my ibex we found he was a fine animal with horns measuring fifty-one and a half inches. While we were skinning him we heard a rumbling roar above us. We knew instantly what it was. Without even stopping to look up, Rahima and the Kazak started running as fast as they could to a buttress of rock that jutted up a short distance away. I paused just long enough to glance in the direction of the noise and saw, silhouetted against the sky, rocks leaping like ibex. For the first time I understood the Psalm "Why hop ye so, ye high hills?" I joined the other two as quickly as I could, and from the safe shelter of the great rock we watched the avalanche churn by taking our ibex with it. A short distance below, on less steep ground, it slowed up and stopped. We gingerly made our way down to it and were delighted to find the head of the animal uninjured. The body skin, however, was so badly torn that it was useless to try to save it. .

I had been carrying around some strychnine to poison the carcasses of such game as we might shoot in order to get specimens of the scavenger birds and animals. This seemed to me an excellent opportunity to use it. While I was putting in the poison I heard a long-drawn whistle. There was Kermit on a neighboring ridge making his way down with his ibex, an animal about the size of mine. He waved to me and evidently wanted to know what I was doing, so I got up and shouted to him. Then I went on with my work. After a few minutes Rahima remarked: "Kermit Sahib and Khalil, they come down." I looked up and, sure enough, Kermit and Khalil were scrambling down the side of the ridge toward us as if they were running a race. I could not imagine why they were doing this, but put it down to exuberance of spirits on the part of Kermit. I remarked to Rahima that it showed what a tough man Kermit was when, at the end of a long hard stalk such as we had just made, he would run down a mountainside for fun. Then we turned again to our work. In a few minutes there was a clatter of rock and Kermit called: "How do you feel, Ted?" I replied in some surprise that I felt perfectly well. It turned out that when I called he had understood me to say I had been poisoned. He had been hurrying down as fast as he could scramble, expecting to find me in a very bad way. Rahima thought it was all a great joke. Kermit naturally did not look at it from that point of view.

Kermit waited until we finished, and we walked down together to the ponies, mounted, and rode to camp through the gathering dusk. We had both shot other and larger ibex, but we were as much pleased with these two as with any. We felt that they had taken hard work and real skill to get, and that is what gives the flavor to shikar.

Next morning the boy we sent out to look at the poisoned carcass came back with an enormous vulture, a lammergeyer. Its body and wings were white shading to buff, except the tips of the wing and tail feathers which were brown shading to black. It measured ten and a half feet from wing-tip to wing-tip. Unfortunately, the Kazak who brought it to camp had used it in part as a saddle, so that it was too much torn to be worth skinning.

Here in the Kargaitash our caravan was a more complete, self-sustaining unit than it had been at any other time. We had a flock of sheep. They were fat-tailed sheep, with a ridiculous bustle of wool on their hindquarters which flounced around as they trotted along. It gave them an even sillier appearance than sheep usually have. On cold nights they coughed exactly like fussy old men. Two or three times I was on the point of asking which one of the men had a bad cold when I realized what it was. We had also a cow and a calf. The former was brought along to give us milk, the latter presumably to share the milk with us. We never found out who came first, but we got little milk and the calf prospered.

In recognition of our letters to the Chinese officials we had an indeterminate guard of Chinese soldiers. We used them for carrying messages. Like all troops of their type, they were always practising petty oppressions on the natives. We would hear sounds of shrill altercation in some village we were passing, and know that something was going on that should not. Then soldiers and villagers would troop out, all talking at once, to lay the case before us. It was difficult to administer justice, for with our very limited means of communication it was impossible to find out just what had happened. Among the soldiers, however, were two good men. The first was a captain, the second in command at Shutta, who joined us as we reached the Kargaitash. He was a good-looking man, tall and slight, with aquiline features. He took a personal interest in our success and was always willing to help. The second was a square-built mustached Kazak named Suffa, who officiated at times as our shepherd. True to his blood, he was a natural hunter, and often pointed out game while we were on the march. As guides we had three Kazak jungli wallahs headed by old Tula Bai, reputed to be eighty-six years old, but as spry as a cricket. We became genuinely fond of all three, and were really sorry to part with them when the time came for them to leave us.

Our pony men came from Aksu. They were a cheerful lot, who almost invariably seemed in a good temper, rain or shine, snow-covered glacier or sunscorched plain. They were very hardy, and I often saw one or more of them stripped to the waist striding along through a snow-storm. Last but not least came our own men whom we had brought with us from Kashmir. The best of these was Rahima Loon, our head shikarry. He had the dignity that is peculiar to the best type of Oriental. He was tall and slight, with a black beard and hawk nose. He knew game and its habits thoroughly. He also had courage. Rarer than all these in the East, he was economical with our money. He unquestionably saved us many hundreds of rupees during the trip. He had been taken to England by one of the "sahibs" with whom he had hunted, and had a general knowledge of the world that far exceeded that of any of the others. He was cautious in his statements and refused to prophesy as to game. When we asked him what we should find in any particular place, he almost invariably would reply: "We go lookum see!"

Fezildin, the dog boy, had changed greatly on the trip. When he came with us he was a timid, unassertive little fellow with the usual Indian pipe-stem legs. He never showed any initiative or mind of his own, but slunk around in the background like a small black shadow. On the way up from Yarkand he began to expand and develop until he had metamorphized into a regular jungli wallah. He discarded his pugri, and blossomed forth in a Turki cap with a fringe of waving black goat hair that framed his face and made him look like the "Wild Man of Borneo" of the circuses. He turned in and helped with the horses and did well. He forded the worst streams without a sign of fear. Indeed, he was generally one of those sent out with a lantern to help Kermit or me when we came back after dark from hunting and had to cross bad water near camp. He was taught skinning, and under the tutelage of Kermit became quite good. His specialty was skinning out the legs, which, next to the head, are the most difficult parts of an animal to prepare. More than all this, when there was work to do he did not have to be hunted out of some corner. Barring the time when poor Foxie died, there was no possible fault to find with his care of the dogs. He was very fond of them and very kind. To hear him when they had done something wrong, however, you would have thought he was an ogre. He bellowed at them like a bull of Bashan, but often while shouting with the utmost ferocity would beat them with a wisp of straw.

Our gamble with the dogs did not turn up trumps. To begin with, the death of Foxie was a severe blow, for we considered him our mainstay. Then there were very much fewer varmints in the Tian Shan than we had anticipated. The bears that Kermit and Cutting shot, and one snow-leopard that we picked up with the glasses some two miles away, were the only ones we saw. In all the hunting that we did, we only came on fresh signs once. As far as the tiger were concerned, we were told that they existed no longer in the Tekkes. Natives are only too willing, as a rule, to say that there is lots of game when there is none, but in this case they all said there were no tiger now. They said that during the last ten or fifteen years the native hunters had killed them off with poisoned meat. Though we tried, we were never able to get the dogs on any varmint trail that was fresh enough to follow. Naturally, this disappointed us, not only because we missed the hunting, but also because we became very fond of the dogs and felt they deserved a chance to make good.

To get good hunting with dogs there should be better conditions than we had, and also a man in the party who gives them constant attention. This man should be an expert on dogs, and should spend his time handling them and searching for country where they will get a chance. Kermit and I were not ex- perts with dogs, and we were far too busy to give them the unceasing attention they needed.

I was not very fluent in Urdu. Kermit was a good deal better than I was, which is merely damn- ing his Urdu with faint praise. Rahima Loon and Khalil spoke English which in quality much re- sembled our Urdu. The result was that at times we had difficulty in understanding each other. This was particularly so when one of the shikaries would try to point out game to us. At best it is hard to see the game they have found. Their eyes are so good that a tiny dot which looks like a rock to the white hunter is recognized at once by them as an ibex. Their favorite method of placing animals was to say in English: "There, just by white e-stone" (stone). As the entire mountain to which they would point was covered with rocks that might have passed as white stones, this was like trying to point out a lark in a meadow by saying it was by a blade of grass. Eventually we would get them to rest the rifle on some rocks and sight it. We would look over the rifle, find the exact spot at which it was pointed, and then search with field-glasses until we found what they had seen.

Sometimes other amusing mistakes occurred.

About four-thirty one cold morning we were getting up to hunt. I was already dressed and had washed in water warmed over the fire. Kermit was still snugly cuddled in his bedding-roll. I had the virtuous feeling common to all on such an occasion, combined as it always is with a rancorous jealousy of his more comfortable condition. In an attempt to be humorous I told the native servant, in my best Urdu, that I wished some cold water to throw over Kermit Sahib to make him get up. A basin of warm water was waiting for Kermit by the tent flap. The native promptly took it away, brought it back filled with ice-cold water from the stream, and solemnly placed it by the washing things. He thought that I had told him that Kermit wished cold water for washing. It seemed an odd taste at four-thirty of a bitter cold morning, but then sahibs are proverbially odd.

All through this region the hawks, vultures, and eagles were numerous. There were generally one or more in sight, floating over the country with far-seeing eyes. Often I lay on my back between stalks, and through my field-glasses studied "the way of an eagle in the air." I agree thoroughly with Solomon thereon, for I have rarely seen anything that approaches these birds in power and effortless grace. At times there would be a gale blowing and they would swoop hither and yon simply by planning, or hold their position over a certain spot by a flickering motion of the wings.

Among the small birds there were pigeons, sparrows, larks, and swallows, but by far the most striking were the black-and-white magpies. There were always two or three flashing about the landscape with that swaggering dandyism peculiar to their breed. I saw them on the grassy hills, in bush-covered slopes, and down among the pine-trees. I watched very carefully and never saw a hawk molest a magpie. Kermit saw a hawk make one unsuccessful attack. The magpies did not seem to be really afraid of the birds of prey. This seemed all the more remarkable, as they are certainly the most conspicuous of birds. They seem to have swaggered themselves into immunity.

The insect life, like the bird life, was not diversified, but in some cases was only too numerous. The chief offenders were the horse-flies. I noticed three species of them. One was like a bee covered with yellow down and corpulent; one like our horse-fly with green eyes; and one the same except for brown eyes. They were most plentiful on the grassy hills. On the slatey peaks of the mountains and in the forest-clad valleys there were comparatively few. They were only active during the sunshiny hours, disappearing like magic when the day clouded over or the sun set. Their bark was considerably worse than their bite. I did not feel them as much as those found in the salt marshes of Long Island, but their numbers and ceaseless buzzing made them at times unbearable. As

Rahima Loon sadly remarked to me after he, like David, had been killing his ten thousands: "Kill one, come three."

In contrast to the horse-flies the butterflies, though numerous, were welcome. They were very lovely and we found them everywhere. There was a deep-red variety with spotted wings that was particularly common. It seemed as if every patch of flowers had one resting on it, its wings moving gently, as if it were breathing. We found other varieties high on the mountains among the slide rock. Those I noticed were more slate gray in color like the rocks, possibly an instance of protective coloration. They had small colored eyes on the wings. A couple of times when I was riding into camp after dark I noticed small white moths in quantities, fluttering about like the fairies of bygone days.

We saw only one species of snake, a small one, twelve to eighteen inches long. It was brown in color, the back banded with darker and lighter stripes. All the men were afraid of them and said they were poisonous. One of our horses that died was killed, we were told, by a bite on the lip from one of them. This we did not believe, but their fangs when dissected did show small poison sacs at the base. As we had left Cherrie our reptile tank with the alcohol, we put two into a bottle of arak given us as a present by an Amban. Taking into account the quality of the liquor, this seemed to us very appropriate.

By this time we had collected the males of all the principal animals that we expected to get in the Tian Shan with the exception of the wapiti, the Asiatic cousin of our elk. It is the largest deer of the Eastern hemisphere. Among living deer it is exceeded in size only by our wapiti. It became known to Western scientists later than the American variety and is named after it, for it is called cervus canadensis songaricus. The mature males weigh between eight and nine hundred pounds. The horns when in velvet are considered a valuable medicine by the Chinese. Large prices are paid for them. In consequence, all the native hunters, Kalmuks, Kazaks and Kirghiz, hunt them continually during the late spring and early summer. All along we had been worried for fear we would not be able to get specimens of this animal, for it is scarce. Indeed, Church in his book written in 1899 considered them to be on the verge of extinction. They are easiest to get when they begin to call. They do not call, however, until the middle of September, and we felt we should start for the Pamirs by that date.

The wapiti live lower down the valley than the ibex and Karelini, so we had to shift camp. We split our caravan, taking with us only the barest necessities, and marched down the Kooksu. Here this river is particularly lovely. Its turbulent and milky waters flow through a rocky gorge. On the south bank the forests run from the edge of the canyon up the hills. Occasionally there is a little grassy meadow. On the north bank the hills are bare and unforested, except where tributary streams run in through similar though smaller gorges.

We camped for the night in one of these small gorges. Through it ran as clear and pretty a brook as any trout-stream of our own North woods. The spruce forest around was virgin. Great fir-trees towered gracefully above us. Beneath them the ground was brown and fragrant with their needles and cones. Here and there the gray dead trunk of some giant tree stretched full length through the undergrowth. On all sides the hills framed us. Magpies flitted saucily around the outskirts of the camp, watching for scraps. The gurgling of the brook sounded ceaseless through all, like the underlying motif in a melody of Mozart's.

The morning after we arrived, Kermit and I shouldered our rifles and went out by ourselves, while Rahima went to look for wapiti sign in a nullah north of camp. We walked down the main river and enjoyed ourselves thoroughly, but saw no game. When we got back to camp it was noon and quite warm. The opportunity seemed heaven-sent. We took our soap and towels and went to the brook for a much-needed bath. The water was icy cold, and in order to get it to cover us we had to lie down on very sharp stones, but we felt like fighting-cocks when we were out drying on "a bar of sun-warmed shingle."

172

When we returned to camp we found Rahima was ready to start. He was far from cheerful. He said he had seen no wapiti signs, and feared that there were very few in the country. We flipped a coin to decide which way each should go. I won, and chose the left branch of the canyon, which seemed the better.

Rahima, a Kazak and I rode up a steep little path to a grassy plateau. From the top we could see the country for miles. The short fragrant summer of the Tian Shan was drawing to a close. The leaves were already turning, and patches of red and brown dappled the green of hillside and valley. To the south, the ridges and snow-crowned mountains stretched like the foam-crested waves of some giant ocean.

We rode up to a point from which we could get a view of the valley, dismounted, and through field-glasses studied woodland and scrub-covered slope. We saw nothing and soon moved on to where we could get another view. Again the result was the same. A cold, drizzling rain was falling when about four-thirty we reached a hill eight or ten miles from camp, from which we could look into a new canyon farther to the west. We were thoroughly discouraged, for so far we had seen the tracks of only one wapiti, and even they were some days old. After we had been searching the country for about a quarter of an hour, Rahima touched me on the arm and said "boogha," Turki for stag. He pointed up the valley.

173

I looked as carefully as I could but was unable to see anything. He said there were two and that they were lying in the bushes. In a moment one of them got up, and I was able to make him out through the telescope. He was a fine big animal of a slate-gray color. He was standing toward the end of a rather broad nullah just beyond a grove of stunted willows.

There was no time to lose, for they were a long way off and darkness was coming. We had a hurried consultation about the stalk. With the wind as it was there seemed to be only one course open, and that was to skirt the small valleys to the right until we came to a slight fold of ground near where they were feeding. It was a long distance—some three miles. We started off at a jog trot along the hillside—Rahima, Tula Bai's son Kassein and I.

Generally I make my shikaries go slowly. All shikaries have far too great a tendency to run their sahib up to the game. This makes the man with the gun shoot when he is out of breath, and multiplies the chance of a miss, for it is possible to be panting only mildly and yet be entirely unable to keep the sight on the target. The shikarry himself, of course, does not notice for he does not shoot. Those who shoot only at a target often wonder why sportsmen miss the shots they sometimes do. The answer is that the sportsman rarely shoots under even approximately good conditions. He is tired or winded, or his position is bad, or he is hurried, or the target

174

is blurred and indistinct. To say "the shooting was done under ideal conditions," is as accurate as the military phrase "at this point the general threw fresh troops into action." No "fresh troops" are ever thrown into a big battle. They are always worn by long marches or lack of sleep, or both. In the same way a sportsman never gets ideal conditions.

This time, however, there was no time to go slowly. It was a question of "Root hog or die!" The three of us hurried over slippery wet hillsides, tripping and falling every few minutes. We climbed over loose rock. We threaded our way between patches of a tall, spiny, cactus-like plant that is common in these mountains. It began to rain in earnest and our clothes became sodden and heavy.

At last, after an hour's hard work, we crept over a rise and saw our game. They had moved up the ravine, and were feeding toward a crest from which the ground sloped into another canyon. There was not a minute to spare, as they were moving. We crawled on all fours to the point we had marked for our shot. They were much farther away than we had expected, and every moment took them still farther. I could not see their horns with my naked eye. They must have been more than 250 yards away, for I paced it afterward and made it 452 of my rather short paces. I was blown, and the rain was beaded on the sights. I raised my rifle, and, taking the most careful aim possible, fired. Fortune tipped my bullet. I saw the stag falter and I knew he was hit. Then I did what I never would have done had I not feared this might be our only chance for wapiti. I switched and fired at the other. Again I was in luck, for the bullet took effect and he staggered. Immediately I switched back to the first, who was slowly making his way up the valley, and with three more shots brought him down. By this time, however, the second animal had gone quite a distance and was moving through the scrub fully 400 yards away. I fired at him a number of times as he showed himself between the bushes. I could get no rest for my rifle as I was on the steep slope of a hill. The range was far beyond any at which I am reasonably sure, and I missed. At last I got Kassein, made him kneel down, and using him as a rest managed to register another hit before the wapiti disappeared over a wooded shoulder. Calling to the men to follow, I started plunging down the hill to trail the wounded animal. The men were far too excited to heed, and ran like lamplighters to where the first animal had fallen in order to hallal him and make him legal Mohammedan food, so I plodded on alone. The jungle was of willow and thorn bushes from four to eight feet high and thickly matted. Beneath them were boulders and cactus-plants. I tangled my rifle in the branches. I slipped and fell. I tore pieces out of both my clothes and myself. To make matters worse, it was now quite dark and I had only two cartridges left. When I reached the crest over which the wapiti had gone, I was blowing like a steam siren. About this time Rahima and Kassein joined me. In a few minutes they pointed out the wapiti some seventy-five yards away. I fired and missed. That left me with one cartridge. I scrambled down the hillside through the deadfall. At times I got a glimpse of a pair of antlers or a broad gray back in the brush ahead, but I did not dare chance a shot, as all my hopes were pinned to that last cartridge. All three of us crashed down through the scrub-willow jungle. Kassein ran ahead. With the usual hardiness of his kind, he seemed as fresh as if he were just starting. By the time we got to the foot of the slope he was well in advance, ranging to left and right like a bird-dog. Well behind, I ploughed along like a very old broken-winded horse with the string-halt. Behind me in turn was Rahima. A shrill whoop from Kassein told me he had our game in sight. Breathless as I was, I could no more have replied than I could have made the proverbial leap over the moon. I headed for him as rapidly as possible, and saw him pointing to a clump of bushes just ahead. Suddenly I found myself within twenty yards of the wapiti, who was looking in the direction of Kassein. My shot took effect, and the fine animal rolled over dead.

One antler of the dead wapiti showed above the grass. For a moment I thought he was a "stag royal," for there were seven tines on this horn, but when I looked at the other I found there were only five tines on it, which made the head a twelve-pointer. The first stag that I had hit was a splendid big animal but had only ten points. Thoroughly happy, I sat down and lighted my pipe.

It was now pitch-dark and raining. Under the circumstances, with the wapiti a mile apart, we could not skin them that night. Kassein took off one of his multitudinous ragged shirts and I took off my leather jacket. We hung these over the carcasses like scarecrows to keep any wolves or scavenger-birds away, and started back to the ponies. When we got to the place we had left them, we found they had strayed, and as far as I was concerned were hopelessly lost. Kassein added to his other admirable qualities owl-like eyes that could see in the dark. He wandered off over the hills, and soon called from the inky black that he saw the ponies. We rounded them up and, shivering but happy, got into the wet saddles.

After two hours' riding we came to the head of the valley where our camp was. Just at this moment the rain stopped, and the moon shone out through the hurrying clouds. The black shapes of the spruce-trees clothing the hillsides contrasted sharply with the bare slopes where the wet grass shimmered in the moonlight. Below us in the valley our camp-fire glowed through the clustered shadows. Rarely have I seen so welcome a sight.

Kermit had seen nothing during the day, so we

178

started early next morning, he to make another attempt to get a stag, I to skin the two I had left in the nullah. Rahima, Kassein, and two of the pony men came with me, with extra horses to carry the heads and hides.

When we got to the valley we found the wapiti undisturbed. In the morning light they looked very big. The larger measured nearly nine feet in total length. This was the ten-pointer, not the twelve-pointer. As so often happens, the size of the horns did not indicate the size of the body. The wapitis' summer coat is red. Their winter coat is gray. The two that I shot had practically completed the change to their winter pelage. They looked to me grayer than our wapiti in the United States, and their antlers seemed less massive.

The men all turned to and helped skin, chattering like monkeys. While they were working I noticed Rahima cut the secretion out of the tear-duct, wrap it carefully in paper, and put it in his pocket. I asked him why he did it, and was told that if a woman mixed it with water and drank it she was sure to be fertile.

We got back to camp about two o'clock. Shortly after, Kermit came in with a good bull wapiti he had shot early in the morning. That gave us all the stags we needed for the museum. The wapiti, which we feared would be very difficult to get, had taken only two days' hunting. The men were delighted, for they were much afraid of the Pamirs in early winter, and knew that this piece of fortune would make it possible to start sooner after the ovis poli.

That evening they built a rousing spruce-wood fire. Its flames danced and flickered in the shadows of the towering evergreens that walled the camp. They squatted around it; the hookah was passed from hand to hand, its gurgle at times audible above the crackling of the logs. Old Tula Bai, his bent form, wagging beard and peaked hat giving him a gnome-like appearance, presided as dean of the Kazaks. Rahima Loon, his eyes gleaming from his dark, clean-cut face, was the central figure among the Kashmiris. The ruddy firelight shining on the bronzed faces threw the whole scene into a bold relief of lights and shadows. Kermit and I drew our chairs up to one side of the fire, smoked our pipes, and listened to stories of stags with great antlers, shot by sahibs whose last trek was made twenty-five years ago.

Having shot our male wapiti, we still had before us the necessary but uninteresting task of getting a female, or maral, as they are called locally, to complete the group for the museum. Rahima Loon, who was a true sportsman, could not quite understand this. He always regarded the fact that we shot females for the museum as a rather serious blot on our otherwise amiable characters. He now suggested that, instead of waiting in the Tian Shan for the maral, we should start back at once for the Pamirs. He explained that there were plenty of female deer in India which we could send the museum for the group. We told him that three male wapiti with a female deer from India would not do. He accepted this rather gloomily as simply an illustration of the weak spot in our intelligence.

After much discussion, we decided that the best way to get maral was to camp at the junction of the Kensu and the Kooksu, and hunt from there. Next morning we moved our baggage-train to this point. In the afternoon we forded the Kooksu and hunted the wooded slopes beyond till dark, without success. When we got back to camp, we found a soldier had arrived from Shutta with a message for us. He also told us that Cherrie and Cutting had been at Shutta for ten days. This put them in the Tian Shan nearly three weeks earlier than had been planned. We had had no letters from them, and we feared something had gone wrong. After talking it over, we decided that we had better go back and join them at once. As for the maral, we would have to try to get it somewhere near them.

Next morning we collected our entire caravan and took to the road again. No one must be deceived by this use of the word "road." A road in the Tian Shan does not bear the slightest resemblance to a road in the United States. It covers anything passable by a clever mountain-pony. The roads here range from the trails across the plains, which are the best, to mountain tracks over glacier and cliff, which take either an ibex or a Tian Shan pony to negotiate successfully.

We pushed on as fast as we could. We crossed a couple of snowy divides, dropped through the spruce-clad foot-hills into the plain, and at the end of the fifth day came to the Moon Tai River. Here we got news that "two sahibs" were in the neighborhood. We camped and sent out men to bring them to us. As we were sitting in front of our tent in the late afternoon, we heard a shout and saw Cherrie and Cutting riding toward us. They both were thin, Cutting particularly so. He was still wearing his enormous regulation British army sun-helmet. In it he looked like a very small candle under a very large extinguisher. We all thoroughly enjoyed our reunion after nearly two months' separation.

CHAPTER VIII

CHINESE TURKESTAN: THE TEKKES TO KASHGAR

WE found that there had been a great deal of friction between the Punjabi and Kashmiri elements in Cherrie's caravan. Fortunately, matters did not reach too acute a point before we joined them. Upon going into the matter we learned that the Punjabis in coming with us had undertaken a separate mission that had become generally known, and it rendered their continuance with us impossible. They were excellent men and we parted with very friendly feeling on both sides.

Cherrie had been sick during the two months that had passed since we left Yarkand. A long-drawn-out bout of dysentery had dragged him down and greatly hampered him in collecting, but his usual pluck had pulled him through.

Suydam had done a great amount of work with his Akeley camera, and was particularly satisfied with what he had taken since coming into the Tian Shan, for he had made pictures of almost every phase of Kirghiz, Kalmuk, and Kazak life. The few days which he had put in hunting had proved amazingly lucky. On the second morning he came upon a she bear and two well-grown cubs—the adult he brought down, but the young ones disappeared into the forest.

This gave us a male and a female bear for mounting in the museum. The following day he saw a large boar. His rifle had acquired a habit of hopelessly jamming, so that it could not be counted upon with any certainty for more than a single shot. In addition the rear sight had been knocked off and was only tied on with string. He took his Kazak shikarry's rifle and fired a couple of times at the boar without result. The boar disappeared into a patch of jungle and after it hurried the Kazak. He killed it with a well-placed shot. Suydam said that he had never seen any animal so fat, and Cherrie estimated the weight at 400 pounds.

Ted and I were now preoccupied with the unromantic task of filling out the groups for the museum with the requisite number of females and young. When one is not hunting an animal, it always seems so much more common and easily attainable. You watch a female ibex and think how simple it would be to shoot one, without, of course, considering an actual stalk and visualizing the difficulties. Then when you are stalking a ram, and a herd of ewes intervenes, you say to yourself how easy it would be if only it were ewes that were in demand. When, however, you set off in cold earnest to shoot a ewe, it is not long before you begin to swing around, and wonder whether, after all, it isn't just as difficult to bring in a female as a male. A long stalk after a female ibex seems much more wearisome, for there is not the same incentive that makes the hard work light. In the accepted ethics of the big-game hunter, there is quite rightly nothing to be proud of in bagging a female, but when you are engaged in scientific collecting the female is of equal importance.

We were much concerned over the prospects for shooting a hind wapiti. We had seen only two; they were running through spruce woods, and the bullets I sent after them were without effect. The upper Mointai was regarded as likely ground, and we planned to have as many strings to our bow as circumstances would permit. Many hunters, when they have wounded an animal and it makes off over particularly rough country, will give a gun to a native shikarry and tell him to follow and finish their quarry; this neither Ted nor I would ever do, so the men were much surprised when we not only did not object to their shooting the group females, but even offered them a reward for so doing. To begin with, they could not understand why we wanted females. We soon gave up trying to explain, and although we thought that Rahima had grasped the situation, our faith was somewhat shaken when he insisted that if we only waited until we were back in Kashmir we could without any difficulty secure several female barasingh which would serve admirably to fill out the wapiti group! Our first attempt after joining Cherrie and Suydam took the form of a very loosely organized drive. It was a lovely day, and the smell

185

of the spruce woods took one back to distant lands and times. On the way out we caught sight of half a dozen black cock, and Ted brought one down with Cherrie's shotgun. The only thing in the drive was a female illik which passed by Suydam's stand and was bagged by Ted. We were in need of it, but there were many around and we had not been at all preoccupied over the difficulties of shooting one. We saw no recent wapiti sign, which was disheartening, for the local Kazaks had felt that they were taking us to their best hunting-ground.

We next went with them to a ridge in the heart of what they considered their best spying land, and we raked the ravine side with our field-glasses, without picking up anything save illik. Two buck were calling; Ted first heard illik calling at Khan Ayalik about the first of September. We had been told that wapiti started about the same time, but this the Kazaks denied, assuring us that they did not begin until the third week in September, and they certainly had not begun when we left the Tekkes around the middle of the month. Discouraged with our failure to find any wapiti sign, we decided to move to Akyas as our last chance.

Cherrie went down to the junction of the Mointai and the Tekkes rivers to put in his last few days collecting in the valley, while Ted, Suydam, and I rode across the rolling prairie to Akyas. Somewhere about half-way we dipped down into a grassy ravine apparently quite like any one of a dozen others through which we had passed. We noticed that the drop was more abrupt, and caught the sound of falling water. We found ourselves in a fairy dingle. A profound and cool cavern, rock-walled and partly screened by tall trees, concealed a deep, clear pool of water, fed by a sizable stream that descended in a shimmery mass through a hole in the rocky roof. Through the hole we glimpsed a patch of blue sky, but within the grotto all was cool and dark. On the grass beneath the trees was charred wood remaining from Kazak fires. We hoped it would be many a day before civilization invades the country and the cavern is strewn with papers and empty sardine cans. What served to make the whole scene particularly refreshing was the unexpectedness of it as we rode unsuspectingly over the plains. The natives call the place Keerkool-douk.

At Akyas we renewed acquaintance with the Russian family and the cheerful small baby, upon whom we bestowed more of the great, gaudy buttons we bought in Paris.

We found that most of the men were down in the valley, making ready the winter supply of hay, a primitive process with sickle and scythe. We managed, however, to gather together a few hunting Kazaks and Kirghiz, among them the two men who had been with Suydam when he shot his bear. Next morning early, taking supplies for a few days, we set off up the Akyas valley, crossing a rough mountain shoulder, where the river had cut its way in a deep and lovely canyon. Above, we followed the widened valley until we came upon a rocky stream which tumbled down into the Akyas from its left bank. A short distance up this tributary we pitched camp amid some tall spruce-trees. Rousslia picked a lot of red berries with a leaf very much like our strawberries. He made them into an excellent shortcake for dinner.

We had no feeling at all about who should shoot the female wapiti. It was a very necessary part of the museum group, but it was essential that we should make all speed possible in order to reach the Pamirs before it became too cold to hunt ovis poli, and we were quite ready to have the maral bagged by Kazak or Kirghiz. We therefore divided up into four groups for the hunting. Suydam took a Kazak; Khalil, to whom I lent my second rifle, went with another Kazak, two more went by themselves, while Ted and I went with Rahima and one native. In addition we offered a reward of about ten dollars to any one who would bring in a maral.

The first hunt proved blank, for although Ted and I saw a couple of wapiti, the wind was gusty, and they were off before we had any chance for a stalk. One of the other groups saw a wapiti but got no shot.

Next morning we were away before daylight, and rode our ponies up toward the mountain tops rimming the valley. Leaving the horses for the long day's doze, we climbed from one vantage-point to another, con-

ning the hillsides and valleys with our field-glasses.
Except for a few illik, we saw no game. At one spot
an interesting engagement took place close to where
I was sitting. A magpie was perched in the top of a
tall spruce-tree, chattering away and admiring itself
in the usual jaunty manner, when all of a sudden
its tone changed and it fluttered hastily over to another dead spruce whose whitened branches were
closely matted together. Simultaneously the shadow
of a hawk flashed across the rocks. He was a brown
fellow but little larger than the magpie. Down he
swooped toward the magpie's refuge, but the branches
were too thick. The chattering magpie hopped
through them to the other side of the tree. Round
went the hawk, and another fruitless dive followed.
This went on for some time; the hawk circled about
in the most graceful of curves; now head down, now
banking, now shooting up. He must have stooped
more than a dozen times, and twice he made a pre-
tense of leaving in order to entice out the magpie.
The latter did not seem particularly frightened; its
cry was not one of alarm, and as soon as the hawk
had really left, he returned to his original perch upon
the solitary tree. He was not destined to enjoy it
long, for almost immediately two brother magpies
came and drove him incontinently away.

The long noon hours when no game was stirring I
passed in reading I and II Samuel.

In the afternoon we separated, Ted and Rahima

going one way, while I took the Kazak Zeytoon and went in the other. We climbed cautiously along an accidented wooded ridge, and had not gone far when, upon reaching the top of a small hill, we saw an illik doe taking her siesta on the far side. We watched her for some time before she even became suspicious. As she jumped to her feet, every motion was an epitome of grace. A few bounds and she stood stock-still. We were careful not to frighten her, for she might alarm whatever was ahead. When she was out of sight, we heard several loud, sharp barks. "Maral, maral," whispered Zeytoon. I thought it was the illik, but Zeytoon insisted it was a wapiti. Topping another rise we again sighted the illik, this time in the act of barking. It seemed a very loud noise to come from so small an animal.

For an hour we held on along the ridge; I had dropped ten yards behind, studying some tracks, when I heard Zeytoon hiss; simultaneously there was a crashing below him on the mountainside. Running on, I caught a glimpse of a wapiti through the scrub willow and spruce. I opened fire immediately, but it was difficult sighting at the maral's fleeting shape through the trees. I was able to get in six or seven shots before she got where I could no longer see her. I felt that I had scored one hit, at least, but Zeytoon was certain I had not. He was so positive that my own belief was badly shaken. Nevertheless, I determined to take a chukker to where I had last seen the wapiti. Before doing so I went on to a lookout point that I had picked out before Zeytoon stirred up the wapiti. Seeing nothing, I returned and dragged a very reluctant Zeytoon down through the fallen timber and the débris of landslides. It was bad going and took time. Farther down we separated to better pick up the trail. Not long after this Zeytoon shouted "She is hit!" and almost simultaneously "Here she is!" I was as much pleased as if it had been a stag. The man who has done all his shooting as a sportsman only, thinks of shooting females much as a man in a fox-hunting country feels regarding any one shooting foxes. But if you have done much scientific work for museums, you come to feel very differently about the distaff side of the groups, and when after a long stalk you bag a female, you have a genuine feeling of satisfaction. I set to work on the measuring and skinning, while Zeytoon went to try to find Ted and Rahima, near where they had agreed to meet us. When he came back with them they were almost as pleased as I had been. To Rahima in particular it spelled a speedy termination of the Tian Shan hunting, and a chance to get into the Pamirs before it became too desperately cold.

Zeytoon set to work with a will to help in the skinning. First he grabbed my rifle and dipped it into the bullet wound, a primitive custom that I had met with among the natives in Africa and Brazil. In pulling off the skin from the back, he seized a fold in his

191

teeth while working with both hands. With such measures we were soon ready, but it was half past seven before we stumbled into camp. None of the other expeditions had seen wapiti, except for Ted. He would have had a shot at a maral had I not fired when I did. She was feeding slowly toward him and would have soon been within close range. On hearing my shooting, she disappeared in a moment. He also saw a male wapiti, an eight-pointer, and could have had a good chance at him had he wished. We had had amazingly good luck with our wapiti. Ted had seen three male and five female wapiti; I had seen one male and five females. Four of the females we had seen while hunting together, so all told we had seen ten wapiti during the week we had been hunting them.

Next morning early we marched back to Akyas, and, picking up the balance of our caravan, shoved on into Shutta, a long trek. On the way we passed through the Kalmuk encampment at Aksu. A wedding was about to take place, and all the inhabitants, gaily dressed, dashed out upon their ponies. The bride was shrouded in a sheet, and was riding double, held on the horse by a man who we were told was her father. Two girls carried a red banner fastened on a couple of tall poles. The gaudy head-dress of the women, the brilliant coats and sashes of the men, the shouting and singing, the wheeling ponies, all combined to make a lively scene. Ted watched them through his field-glasses as they rode off down the plains toward the Tekkes. He saw the women and men divide into different groups, and then the carrying off of the bride was enacted, for her husband dashed in among the women and seized her and bore her away on his horse.

A group of Kazak graybeards whom we shortly afterward met amused us. There were six of them, and each held a small grandson in front of him on the saddle; the children were, some of them, scarcely more than a year old, chubby and solemn. We had seen similar cavalcades before; verily the children are brought up on horseback!

At Shutta our friend the Dauran came out to greet us. Cherrie had dressed the abscess in his back, cleaning it out and putting powdered calomel into it. The treatment, although both novel and drastic, had been most successful and he was now well. He did his best to persuade us to stay over a few days in Shutta, and when we with much difficulty convinced him of the impossibility of our doing so, he said that he would come on with us as escort next day. All the soldiers wished their photographs taken, and Loya brought out his two pretty wives and his roly-poly son. There was a young illik in one of the compounds, very friendly and wandering everywhere at will. He was, however, not so eager to pose for his portrait as were the soldiers.

We planned to complete the ibex group at Khan

Ayalik. We did not have the same concern about our ability to do so as in the case of the wapiti. We felt reasonably certain that with some hard climbing and lucky shooting we could secure the female and young without unreasonable delay. It was on the 13th of September, Ted's birthday, that we set off for the mountain tops—Ted, Suydam, and myself, with Khalil and two Kirghiz. Rahima stayed in camp to pack the skins and horns for the crossing of the Muzart glacier.

We went up along one of the side glaciers where Rahima and I had put in our first day after ibex. The elapsed six weeks had wrought great changes; there was more snow on the mountains and the flowers had almost completely disappeared. We were not long in picking up a herd of females; they were well up among the rocks and the wind was tricky, necessitating a long détour and a good deal of climbing. I had had an attack of fever hanging over me for the last three days; with the help of plenty of quinine I had managed to head it off, but I was not feeling up to much.

It was impossible to get within good range, and the nearest animals were 250 yards distant when at last we were in a position to fire. We had spread out behind a ridge, and though the range was long, fortune favored us so that when we came to count heads we had a half-grown male, two females, and two young. This topped off our big males and gave us a really admirable group. We got the measuring and skinning finished with all despatch, but it was well after dark before we reached camp.

We found Cherrie waiting for us; he had had a most successful few days collecting along the banks of the Tekkes. Ted now took over the small-mammal trapping, and until we again separated at Maralbashi, every night, no matter how late we got to camp, nor how rainy and cold it might be, he set out twenty traps. Often he would have to take with him a lantern when he was laying out the line, but in spite of it all he added much exceedingly valuable and interesting material to the collection.

Ted and I had worn shorts throughout the whole trip; they give free action for the knee and help immensely where there is much climbing to be done. Your knees soon become so tough that they are as impervious to cold, as is your face. We each had flannel shirts and leathern waistcoats, and I wore a canvas coat with many pockets, for I always carry a varied assortment of odds and ends with me when I am hunting. The best footgear for mountain work is the grass shoe; with it you can walk more noiselessly and surely than with anything else, but unfortunately its life is too short to make it practicable, except when you are in its home country. I wore Kashmir chuplies —a heavy sandal over a light leathern sock—a good deal, and found them satisfactory except when they got wet; then they slipped about from under your foot and were worse than nothing. They had another disadvantage in that small stones often became wedged in between the sock and the sandal. I had brought with me a pair of boots with corrugated rubber soles. Hitherto no rubber shoe had lasted me long when hunting, and I placed but little confidence in these. The soles usually ripped off before long. This time I was agreeably surprised, for these crepe-soled shoes stood up admirably under the roughest kind of treatment. They were noiseless and gave a good grip upon rock and hillside. In headgear we had made several shifts. From Srinagar the whole way to Aksu we wore helmets, for of course they are the only thing to wear when you have reason to fear the "sun overhead." Thereafter for the marching we adopted the Kashmiri puggree, or turban; very comfortable and much more suited than a helmet for travel in an araba. While hunting, Ted wore a balaclava helmet, and I had an old corduroy cap which Mr. P. B. Van der Byl had given me in London. We had been indebted to him for much friendly advice and help drawn from his store of experience gathered in the big-game haunts of every quarter of the globe.

On the 14th of September we crossed the Muzart Pass, a very different crossing from that we had made on the 2d of August. Now we had glorious weather, with the bright sunshine dancing on the snowy peaks and ice ridges. We were evidently in the height of the caravan season. On the way from

Shutta we had wound through three great flocks of sheep, totalling 3,000 head. The buyers came from Aksu and bought on the hoof, hiring the wild Kalmuk and Kazak herdsmen to drive the animals over the passes. We also saw a big herd of ponies, and innumerable caravans of donkeys. These later seemed to have the preference as pack-animals on this route. The little beasts in the main were loaded with great bales of cotton and cloth and felt numdahs. We passed over the long glacier without incident, although there were a number of moments when it looked as if we would lose a pony; one in particular I made sure had fallen into a crevasse, but he recovered himself in miraculous fashion. A cold rain set in just as we reached the other side, but we soon had our tents up and could retire into them with the comfortable feeling that the Muzart Pass lay behind us.

Next day we continued down the Muzart River on the opposite side from that we had ascended, for all was changed here as well as on the pass, and we had no longer dangerous fords to deal with. We spent our first night at Khailak, where I was very busy going over the last lot of ibex skins and putting all the additional touches that you never seem to finish to your own satisfaction. We went on past the Chinese wall where we had previously pitched our camp and stopped at the little village of Kizil Bulak. As we arrived, a cheerful little Beg came up to greet us. He had come with us as a passenger from Yarkand to Aksu and brought us out our mail to Jam when we were going into the Tian Shan. Once again Sadi, for that was his name, appeared in the rôle of Mercury, and never was more welcome than when he produced a great packet of letters from the folds of his robes. According to invariable custom, everything else stopped happening as suddenly as it had in the palace of the sleeping Princess, while each took his letters and retired to the nearest shady spot to read them. When you are off on a hunting trip, especially in a far country, the really formidable fly in the ointment is your continuous anxiety as to how things are going with your family at home, and letters help immensely even if they do not bring you very close to date. We could not have been any farther away or more cut off from communication than we had been. I had tried using the Chinese telegraph-line, sending a message to a friend in Peking and asking him to relay it to New York. My telegram took eighteen days to get from Aksu to Peking!

Another old friend who rode in to see us was Ismail Bey, the big local landowner, who had helped us so greatly on our way over into the Tekkes. We were genuinely glad to see him again, for he is a fine fellow. Our men always pronounced Bey as Boy, and referred to Ismail as Big Boy, in contradistinction to a Bey from Khan Ayalik who had come across with us. The latter they called Little Boy. At first we were much puzzled as to whom they meant by Big

198

and Little Boy. The confusion further increased when by a process of elision Ismail Bey's name was made to sound as if it were Small Boy.

In the morning we rode over with Ismail Bey to his little oasis, where he lived in a true patriarchal style with a stalwart old father and numerous brothers and sisters. The buildings were many and well kept. We would like to have accepted his invitation and stayed a few days with him. He had a big hooded eagle which we would have been glad to see in action, but time pressed far too heavily to admit of delaying. Ismail gave us a very fine riding pony, for he did not approve of the one that I was riding, and when we parted we gave him Ted's Springfield, for he was now using his Hoffman entirely.

The Bey came on to Arbat with us, in order to arrange a goitred-gazelle hunt. We were eager to get a group of the graceful little creatures for the museum, provided it did not entail too much time.

We had heard that there were a few sheep in the hills near by. Church, in his book, mentioned seeing three; we had not been so fortunate, but when Cherrie had come through he also had seen three and Cutting had gone after them. We would have given much to have had two weeks in which to hunt these sheep and determine just what they were. There is a most interesting field open in the study of the great Asiatic sheep. Some one should follow them straight down from where they are found near northern Mongolia not far from Peking to the Altai Mountains, the home of the ovis ammon typica, and then throughout the length of the Tian Shan range, where there are the Karelini and very probably one, or possibly two, undescribed species. Next he should go to the Pamirs, collecting Littledale's sheep on the way, and after getting ovis poli finish with ovis ammon hodgsoni in Changchemmo and western Tibet. It would indeed be an interesting study to trace the intergradations, from the great wide-spreading horns of the poli to the heavy close-curled head of the ammon typica.

Ismail Bey had arranged a drive for gazelle in the foot-hills, so early in the morning we rode down to our stations. Four men did the driving. Three does came by me travelling like the wind, and I knocked one of them over at a very close range.

We tried another drive but nothing came through, so Ted and I separated and started off across the plains to hunt our way toward Jam, whither the caravan had preceded us. We each of us saw about a dozen gazelle, but they were exceedingly wary. I don't believe I got within 800 yards of one of them. At that distance they would start moving off, with gradually increasing speed, and to follow them was but a vexation of the spirit. Unless for the luck of a chance shot, the most likely place to hunt them would be in the foot-hills, where you would have some hope for a stalk. The heat-waves shimmered and danced over the barren rocky floor of the desert, but as I got down to the oasis the twilight was coming on, and in its magical fashion lending an austere charm to even the bleak country through which I was riding.

Another day brought us to Aksu, where we were greeted by our friend the Dotai. He pressed us to stay over for four or five days, but we were adamant, and compromised on invitations by asking him to dine with us, and agreeing to breakfast with him in the morning, and leave immediately afterward on our trek to Kashgar. Both affairs were as pleasant as possible. The Dotai was much interested in the ibex and sheep heads, and we dispensed with interpreters as much as we could by using the sign-and-sound language, which Ted supplemented by drawing pictures of the events of the chase, to the great delight of all our friends. When we told of the bear-hunt the Dotai growled and waved his hands most dramatically. At another time, in order to explain the nature of the soup we were having at his breakfast, he flapped his hands and quacked. Altogether every one had a fine time, and the Dotai took particular pleasure before the breakfast in showing us over his flower-garden, where there was every imaginable flower, most of them in full bloom. In one corner of the garden there was a Yarkand stag in a pen, a handsome animal but distinctly short-tempered, in which it was quite different from another Yarkand stag that had been brought around to our camp in the hope that we might buy it. This last was tame and friendly, although its horns were just coming out of the velvet, and at that time stags are usually in bad humor. We were told of the different localities in which these deer had been caught, and our informants spoke as if they were in no way uncommon. Once more we wished we had a couple of extra weeks in hand.

Some of our Shutta bodyguard had accompanied us to Aksu. They were a far finer, more soldierly lot than any we met with on the plains. Our men referred to them as "Peking" men, although of the two best soldiers we had in the Tian Shan, one was a Kirghiz, and the other, although he called himself Chinese, his "father's father knew it not." Calling them "Peking" men reminded me of how Father found the Indians with whom he hunted in the Cœur d'Alene region in Idaho still calling Americans "Boston men," in contradistinction to the Canadian trappers who were French.

We couldn't get away from Aksu until one o'clock in the afternoon of the 12th of September, but the evening of the 24th found us at Maralbashi. If you load your arabas not too heavily, you get across the country surprisingly speedily. We had a fairly large assortment of books with us, but the only good araba books were Cumberland's "Sport in the Pamirs" and Ted's copy of "Omar Khayyam." In all the other books the print was too fine. Naturally enough, when you select books for a hunting trip, size is a primary consideration, and size and large type rarely go together. I found Green's Hindustanee Grammar a good araba companion, for in studying you do not read so closely and continuously. One can read and enjoy books in the wilds which at home would never occur to you to take on. In this class we put Meredith's "Egoist," a small pocket edition of which kept me in reading matter for a number of weeks. When in addition to hunting you are writing articles and preparing museum specimens, you have not very much time to read. Our library covered a large range of taste; in the Tian Shan I read, besides "The Egoist," "Westward Ho," "Pickwick Papers," "Jorrocks Jaunts," and the "Romany Rye." We had brought two volumes of collected poems; one was Kipling and the other Edwin Arlington Robinson. Into them we would constantly dip, and they proved admirable companions. They never went back in the yakdans, but travelled in our bedding-rolls.

We found many changes in the plains. Instead of the great heat at midday, it was now only pleasantly warm, and marching was more agreeable in consequence. There is a great abundance of fruit in Turkestan. The apricot season had passed, but in its place were peaches and grapes and delicious melons of many kinds. In addition to the red-fleshed watermelon, there was one with yellow flesh. I could detect little difference in taste. Then there were various sorts of muskmelon. Every one was eating melons; we saw one small boy clad in the altogether eating a huge slice. He was covered with a thick coating of dust, and down his whole length the trickle of the juice had ploughed deep furrows.

Along the roadside squatted melon venders, and our araba drivers were continually purchasing the fruit and sharing the slices among themselves. When we halted at some dreary little serai in the middle of the desert, we greatly enjoyed the big watermelons.

In some of the gardens where we camped there were walnut-trees. The nuts were now ripe, and our host would knock them from off the trees for us.

One march short of Maralbashi we left Cherrie and Suydam to spend a few days near some swampy lakes where we hoped they would add some interesting material to the birds and small mammals already forming the collection. This promised to be a long parting, for if all worked out as planned, they would return through Russia, and we would next meet in New York, a far cry from the swamps of Maralbashi.

In Maralbashi we changed a couple of our arabas and redistributed the loads. We got there on a Thursday, which is market-day, and as we rode in we passed swarms of peasants returning from the bazaar. One mother was holding a small child on the saddle in front of her, a larger one was astride the pony's quarters, clasping his mother round the waist for support. An old couple were driving in a donkey-cart, the first we had seen, and built on the lines of an araba. Women were trudging along with children strapped on their backs, nodding and asleep after the excitement of market-day.

There was still a lot of life in the bazaar; it was just before the regular night life had started, and belated knots of country people yet lingered. Two old men were playing chess, with Chinese chessmen, which are just like checker-men, and are distinguished one from another by the ideographs carved on them. Sometimes you find fine ivory sets, yellowed with age and use. The moves are much the same as in the chess we play. An interested crowd of onlookers were offering voluble advice.

We were eager to get through to Kashgar in four days, and to do so called for daily marches of little short of forty miles. In the Orient stray individuals have a way of attaching themselves to caravans in the desire of making a journey with more security and economy; they also enjoy the advantages of companionship, and can sit up all night chattering and then sleep at odd moments during the day, a practice to which the Oriental is much addicted. We still had with us Sadi, the little Yarkandi; so far as we could find out he was travelling around with us for amusement; he understood a little Hindustanee and made himself useful in a thousand ways. He was invariably bright and cheerful at the end of the longest march. We had also a solemn Chinaman who had joined us at Shutta. He was evidently a humorist in his way and was a source of continual amusement. He had a very loud voice and would hop out of his araba when any wrangle started, and they were not infrequent; with many gesticulations and loud bellows he would champion whatever he took to be our cause; but his entering in served only to prolong the argument, so he would be hauled away and put back in his araba.

The trail from Maralbashi to Kashgar we found very hot and dusty. There was much desert, some of it barren and stony, and some of it covered with scrub-tamarisks. When you walked you sank ankle-deep in dust; it felt as if you were treading on sponge-cake. Hair and beard turned gray, and dust filled our bedding-rolls. We had a new moon and toward night we would begin to enjoy the march, for desert and jungle became mysterious and eerie by moon-light. We usually marched for twelve or fourteen hours, unspanning for an hour or two at noonday.

At Faizabad, our halt the night before reaching Kashgar, a pleasant, thin little Chinaman, the Amban, came to call, and greatly surprised us by addressing us in English. He knew but a few words which he had learned years before in Peking. He proved most considerate by staying only a few minutes, for it was ten o'clock when we reached town and we were ready for supper and bed.

Next morning we hired riding ponies in order to ride into Kashgar ahead of the arabas, and while waiting for the horses to be made ready I strolled through the bazaar; there were many prosperous-looking shops. Hearing some singing, I loitered toward it. A sturdy fakeer in a white-and-gold embroidered robe, with his begging-bowl strapped to his waist, was striding along, followed by his three sons, ranging in age from six to twelve. They were well-set-up boys, cleanly dressed, and with snowy-white turbans. Father and sons had nothing cringing about them, nor were they, on the other hand, insolent; they appeared merely independent and self-respecting. At almost every shop something was put into the big bowl. What was most remarkable, however, was the singing; the father sang the verse and the sons joined in the choruses. It was totally unlike any Oriental music I have ever heard; indeed, the whole sounded more like what Meredith describes as "one of those majestic old Gregorian chants, that wherever you may hear them, seem to build up cathedral walls about you." There was a glorious swing to it, which the father brought out, beating the cadence by the raising and lowering of a muscular arm. I would have liked to have known the history of the little band, but could learn nothing of it.

The muezzins were calling the faithful to prayer as we rode into Kashgar. We were greeted by the Dotai and other Chinese officials, who had a most elaborate tea prepared for us in a terraced garden where stood the Dotai's summer-house. Thence we went on to the British Consulate, where Major and Mrs. Gillan welcomed us with an understanding hospitality. I had known Gillan in Mesopotamia during the war.

The bazaar in Kashgar proved far more interesting than that in Yarkand. Thursday being market-day, the country folk thronged in from miles around. The silk and cloth bazaar, all roofed over, was gratefully cool. One could not help being struck with the handsome features and dignified bearing of the venders as they sat among their wares. The twisting alleyways of the boot bazaar were dim and mysterious. Never have I seen so much footgear gathered into such a small compass. The sellers were pursuing customers through the crowd, endeavoring to persuade them to raise the purchase price which they had offered. The hat bazaar seemed to hold enough caps to cover every head in Turkestan; some of the caps were elaborately embroidered in gold and fur-trimmed.

In leisurely fashion, as befitted the occasion, I wended my way through the fruit and vegetable quarters and into the squares where squatted the kabab-sellers, with chunks of mutton strung on small skewers roasting over their charcoal fires. If you felt hungry you silently selected a skewer, and, buying a piece of unleavened bread, pulled off the meat and ate with the bread for plate. Roast ears of corn were also popular.

It was in the job-lot bazaar that I lingered longest.

Here was spread out every imaginable thing: bits of broken iron, lovely jade snuff-bottles, old tin cans, altar ornaments of the Buddhist faith, long daggers with turquoise studded handles, empty cologne-bottles, old Chinese locks, copper jugs of every shape, and a thousand and one heterogeneous odds and ends.

At length I found my way to the Hukta, an enclosed garden in the centre of the town, not unlike a very large patio in a South American house. The sheltered platforms beneath the walls were crowded with sweetmeat sellers. Under the trees there were four or five groups listening to story-tellers. In the middle of one gathering two men were telling a story in dialogue with much gesticulation; near by a man was holding forth alone, but making up in vehemence for the lack of a companion. A venerable-appearing old man was reading aloud, and his listeners were mostly graybeards. He never raised his eyes as I and my native followers came up, and paid no attention whatever when one of my men peered over his shoulder to see what it was he was reading. The fact that his listeners showed much interest in us disturbed the tenor of his reading not a whit. Not far away another old man was entertaining a numerous group by reading from the "Elf Leila Wa Leila"—the "Thousand and One Nights." In town we found copies of this classic in Arabic, Persian, and Turki.

Within hearing of the story-tellers and in the shade cast by a row of elms, half a dozen men were busy massaging clients. At the invitation of a cheerful old fellow I spread myself upon his quilt, and enjoyed an excellent massage, while a small naked child sat beside me, occasionally joining in with a thump in emulation of the work of his elder.

We were glad to leave Kashgar, for it meant that we were launched on the homeward stretch with our faces toward Kashmir, but I shall long remember the many pleasant hours we spent with our friendly and long-suffering hosts at the Consulate, and the careless rambles through the bazaar.

CHAPTER IX

THE PAMIRS AND THE POLI

"And now there came both mist and snow
And it grew wondrous cold."
—COLERIDGE.

WE stayed four days at Kashgar, and gathered ourselves for the last effort of the trip—our hunt for ovis poli. Round the horns of this great sheep, story and legend have clustered for ages. Forgotten for six hundred years after Marco Polo first noticed him, he was rediscovered in the late thirties of the last century by a British officer. Since then he has been the lodestar of big-game hunters. We could get but little late news of him. Indeed, many of those best posted considered the ovis poli nearly extinct.

During these four days we replenished our supplies, and packed the heads and skins to be taken out by Cutting and Cherrie. These two were following us more slowly, collecting as they travelled. At this point our trails finally split, as they planned to go out through Russia.

Every one was kind and helpful. Major Gillan, the British Consul, did all in his power to aid us. The Dotai, the Chinese Governor of the province, also was most kind. He was a cheerful old boy with a plump, round face like a russet apple. We exchanged the usual formal calls, our dinner-jackets making their last appearance.   Mrs. Gillan did her best to make them moderately presentable, but they were too far gone. In spite of her efforts, we looked like dissipated waiters in a third-class restaurant on the Bowery.

The social round finished with a luncheon given us by the Dotai on the day of our departure. At the luncheon were the official family of Kashgar. The talk turned on the long-haired tiger. The Chinese General, a fine-looking old fellow with a strong, clean-cut chin, told us how some twenty years before, a tiger was supposed to have jumped into an araba just outside of Maralbashi. The driver jumped out as the tiger jumped in, evidently feeling that in this case two was not company but a crowd. The horses then bolted and dragged the tiger through the city and out the other side. Other stories followed of much the same type, interesting but suggesting Munchausen rather than George Washington. As a matter of fact, we found that none of the company had ever seen a tiger, alive or dead, and that their information was mere hearsay.

After the meal was over, we took off our draggled finery, put on our hunting-clothes, and rode after our caravan. It had started off in the morning, so we did not catch up until night.

With our pony caravan there were, as usual, two Chinese soldiers. This time, however, they were better men, or the natives of the country were of a higher social status, for there were no cases of oppression with which to deal. Our head pony man was a draggled old gray-bearded Beg, who looked like Time in a primer. He wore a long, faded red wrapper, which flapped around his thin shanks in the bitter mountain wind like a torn sail round spars in a gale. He fluttered along behind the caravan like a piece of paper in a windy city street. Last but not least was Rah Tai Koon Beg, a fat, bearded, jolly fellow, with a bright-blue coat belted in with a yellow scarf. Very often he rode with us and carried one of the rifles. The rifle-sling was not long enough to suit his figure, and the rifle was half hidden in the clothes and fat that covered his broad back.

For a couple of days we travelled through the plains. We passed from oasis to oasis. Burned and forbidding, the desert lay between. There was an endless succession of scrub bushes and sun-scorched rock, with dust-devils dancing between. Time and again we passed small oases on which the desert was marching. On their outskirts were houses half buried in sand, and dead trees whose gray, gnarled upper limbs alone stuck out of sand-dunes. Closer in, where the sand had not yet conquered, were half-submerged fields and partially covered trees whose tops were still green with leaves.

On the third day we turned due south. Soon we were among the foot-hills. The plains of Turkestan were behind us.

Turkestan, though it has been comparatively civilized for a long time, has changed but little in the last thousand years. The leaders still practise mediæval directness in dealing with those they dislike. Last year the General at Kashgar became too efficient and raised too large an army. The Governor of Turkestan descended on Kashgar unannounced, and the General's head presently appeared over one of the gates of the city.

Perhaps the most unpleasant sight we saw in this country were the prisoners. The state considers that it has done its duty when it has thrown them into prison. It does not provide them with food. They are led each day to the gates of the city, chained there, and left to beg their food from charitable passers-by. Mowing and gibbering in their chains, their wild eyes peering from beneath their tangled black hair, their gaunt limbs showing through the filthy rags in which they were clothed, they were a gruesome sight.

The hills were more than welcome after the long weeks we had spent in the plains. Bare and red, they suggested the buttes of Colorado. We marched up the bed of a rocky stream, the trail weaving from side to side over numerous fords. About noon we saw two men approaching on horseback, who turned out to be Nadir Beg and the mail-runner from India.

Nadir Beg was the native that Gillan had got us as a guide for the ovis poli country. He was an important citizen of the town of Tashkurgan, a fine-looking man with a light complexion, a black beard and a hawk-like nose. He was a Sarikol, one of a people who live in the valleys and mountains of that name. These Sarikoli, because of their Aryan features and light complexions, are said to be descendants of the soldiers of Alexander the Great, whose "distant footsteps" still echo down the corridors of time in northwestern India. In the East, where nothing is entirely forgotten, and little remembered with accuracy, the tradition of the great Macedonian remains as the myth of a demigod.

That evening we camped by a little Kirghiz settlement on a small plain in the valley. The principal building was a mud-walled square around a great cottonwood-tree. In it was bivouacked a caravan from Tashkurgan on its way to Kashgar. The men were good-looking lean fellows and very friendly.

Around the camp-fire we worked out our plans for the poli-hunting. Nadir Beg said that though goolja (rams) were scarce, he had seen a fine head shot by a Kirghiz near Subashi the previous winter. We accordingly decided to try that point first.

For the next two days we pushed on up the river. At times the trail was very bad. It wound along the steep sides of the mountain. The valley narrowed into a gorge through which the stream rushed so rapidly that fording was very difficult. A small boy, perhaps fourteen years old, led the head pony of our

215

caravan. At one of the fords he fell in, but was pulled out by Nadir Beg and some of the others. After the water had been tilted out of him he seemed all right. His clothes, however, could not be worn wet in the bitter cold, so he was fitted out from various surplus stores. As he was by all odds the smallest of the party, the fit was far from good. The final touch to his attire was given by an enormous pair of knee-high boots which made him look, as he paddled along, like the Puss-in-boots of the fairy-tale.

After crossing the ford where the boy fell in, I noticed the head pony man stoop down and put a stone on a small pile that was there. That was Tauism, or nature-worship. The people of this country are nominally Mohammedans, but, like most people who live in the lonely places of the world, their religion is largely overlaid with primitive nature-worship. Wherever there was a bad ford we saw these piles of rocks. At times we saw trees with bits of rag or paper fluttering from their branches.

At one place we were delayed many hours because a part of a bridge had been destroyed. Before we could get the caravan over, we had to rebuild much of the road. Even then it took the efforts of three or four men, pushing and pulling, to get each pack-pony across. Just beyond, on the other side of the river, there were holes sunk in the rocks. I asked Nadir Beg what they were. He told me they were the remains of a bridge built in Yakoob Beg's time. Yakoob Beg was a very competent Mohammedan who headed a successful revolt some sixty or seventy years ago. He ruled in Turkestan for a number of years. It was only after his death that China regained her control. I noticed that improvements and public works were very often credited to him by the natives. It would seem that he must have been a very able man, but perhaps it is only a case of the far hills being the greenest.

As we wound our way along, we met an occasional caravan moving toward the plains. The men were generally so bundled up that they looked like animated bolsters. A number of times we noticed poliskins, either on their saddles or covering their bales. This encouraged us very much. When we questioned them they told us that these were the skins of arkal (female sheep) from both the Chinese and the Russian Pamirs.

Sometimes we came on great woolly Bactrian camels, which lifted their heads from their grazing and eyed us incuriously. They were in splendid shape, fat and strong. It was a constant source of wonder to us that these great animals were able to keep in such good condition feeding on the withered bushes and scant dry grass of the country.

Here we saw a type of shelter we had not seen before, a mud-and-stone yourt. The bottom was built of rough rocks, the top was of dry clay. Generally they clustered in the lee of some large rock, like chickens around a hen.

One bitter cold morning Loosa brought in a small

gray mouse that he had caught in his hands. It was a new species so Kermit conscientiously skinned it, though skinning is far from pleasant when the steel cleaves to your hands from cold.

One afternoon as we were riding along we noticed a hawk pursuing a large blue rock pigeon. The latter took refuge in a hole in a crumbling mud-bank by the side of the trail. Nadir Beg and Fezildin galloped up, and a chase for the pigeon started. They scrambled down and tried to catch it by reaching into the hole where it had gone. It was really very heavy odds, for whenever they scared the pigeon out of the hole the hawk would swoop at it. At last, I am glad to say, it got off scot-free, eluding all pursuers, bird and man alike, and disappeared behind a cliff.

It had now begun to be bitterly cold. The snow lay thick on the mountains. Snow flurries and sleet-storms swept across the valley nearly every afternoon. The wind blew with gusty fury. At night the tin cup of water that Kermit and I had left between us in the tent froze solid. As the trees and large bushes had all disappeared, our fires consisted nearly entirely of yak dung, with occasionally a few scrub-bush roots called burtsa by the natives. Yak dung burns with a pungent odor that is rather pleasant. It serves only for cooking, and does not warm you when the weather is really cold. It is one thing to camp in our own North woods where fuel is plentiful, and where, when the hunter comes in chilled and tired, he builds a roaring fire of birch and pine; but it is a very different matter in the Pamirs, when he arrives in camp to no fire at all. We went to bed immediately after getting to camp, for it was the only place where we could be reasonably comfortable. Even there all we could do was to lie still and think, for it was too cold to hold a book even if a candle could be kept alight in the wind. Getting up in the gray light of early morning was also far from pleasant. Everything was frozen. Very often the snow was deep outside of the tent. Every piece of clothing was damp and cold. As time wore on, we took off less and less when we went to bed, until the phrase "undressed for the night" might better have been changed to "dressed for the night."

The evening of the fourth day out we reached Bulun Lake. Our caravan had been travelling very slowly, and we had decided to speed it up. Accordingly, we marched ahead and told the leaders not to stop until they caught up with us. We reached the lake just before dusk. There was but little water in it. Indeed, it consisted mainly of sand-bars with shallow channels between. At sunset the brown of the sand, set off by the shining winding strips of water, made the whole seem like some gigantic placque of bronze inlaid with silver.

It was after dark when we reached the small settlement that goes by the name of Bulun. In the gloom we saw the shadowy shape of a square, half-ruined mud fort, with a few yourts clustered around it. After much chattering of shadowy figures that flitted through the dark, we got off, and were shown into one of the yourts to await the arrival of the caravan now well behind us.

Inside the yourt a Kirghiz family was gathered around the dung fire, which cast a glow rather than a light upon them. There were the man, his wife, a rather handsome, worn woman, and three brown, bright-eyed children, who sat as quiet as little mice. The air was so filled with smoke that it was almost impossible to keep our eyes open. This is the way these Kirghiz must spend fully twelve to fourteen hours a day through many of the winter months. There was neither room nor light in the yourt to do anything. I do not believe they think much, so like the North country farmer, I suppose they "just set."

We and our men crowded in, completely filling the yourt. We were very grateful for the shelter from the wind, and the comparative warmth from the huddled humanity and the tiny fire. When the caravan arrived some hours later, we were sorry to have to go to our flimsy canvas tent.

Next morning we were up at daylight. The lake was cupped by snow-covered hills. Frost lay heavily on the brown sparse grass. Suddenly, through a gap in the mountain wall, a great level ray of sunlight fell, painting the low-lying clouds gold. A flock of ducks flew over, their wings flickering in the golden morning light.

While the cold-stiffened ponies were being caught and loaded, I noticed the old, white-bearded Beg in charge of the pony-train standing near a building around which swallows were flying. Unexpectedly he stretched out his hand and caught one as it flew by. He looked at it for a second and then threw it into the air, and away it sailed. Though these swallows swooped very close to me, it would have been impossible for me to have duplicated his feat. Unfortunately, as our ability to communicate with the natives was, to put it mildly, limited, I was unable to find out whether this was the first time he had done anything of the sort, or whether he was in the habit of doing it.

We marched to the Little Kara Kul, where, after talking with the natives, we decided to stop and hunt for a day. The village of Little Kara Kul consisted of a stone kraal in which are three or four yourts. We were now in the land of the yak again, and the great shaggy beasts grunted and shuffled around our tent all night.

A yak is not an uncomfortable animal to ride, but patience is necessary. He goes very slowly though his gait is reasonably smooth, and he always gets there. Also, he goes over the most impossible country imaginable about as fast as he goes over level ground. He plods unconcernedly through snow up to his belly, or up a boulder-strewn slope of forty-five degrees. He moves over obstacles with the same deliberate unconcern with which I have seen a tank in the war negotiate a shell-hole. He is guided with a rope through his nostrils, and steers like a dray. He blows like a porpoise, keeps his mouth open a large part of the time, and lolls a long ant-eater-like tongue from side to side. I have seen a small icicle form from the saliva on the tip of his tongue, but could not see that it inconvenienced him at all. Once we rode our yaks into a valley where there was a herd of the same animals. The beast I was riding began to give curious throaty bellows. The old bulls of the herd at once waltzed up, holding their tails in the air like feather dusters. They made no attempt to attack, but played around us like ungainly puppies. There were dust wallows near by in which the great shaggy creatures would lie and roll.

When we got up next morning it was bitterly cold. The sky was the monotonous gray of winter. Everything was white from a light snow. After a hurried breakfast, we started for the hunting-grounds, mounted on yaks. Their black woolly backs were in-crusted with frost. On the first lake we passed a flock of geese settled, spiralling down from the sky with a musical honking. They stood in a row on a sand-bar like sentinels. The next lake was frozen except at one end. In the open water were myriads of ducks and geese. As we came up they rose into the air with a sound like ocean surf on a shingle beach.

It was typical Pamir country, sandy valleys dotted with tufts of dried grass, and snow-covered hills and mountains. For so barren a country there was a surprising amount of wild life. We saw snow-buntings, pigeons, vultures, and hawks. There were many tracks across the snow. I noticed much wolf sign, tracks of marmots, tracks like those of some small cat, and the trail where a little mouse had run hither and yon, dragging its tail in the snow, evidently in search of roots. We flushed four or five large hares which loped off with deceptive speed. To the latter Kermit and I, mindful of the old Southern custom, solemnly took off our caps in order that we might have luck with the poli.

As we were plodding along, Khalil jumped off his yak, calling out "goolja!" and pointing to a slope some 600 yards away. Along it were running two small poli rams, with horns about twenty inches long. They were too small to shoot, but it gave us a thrill to see the ovis poli in the flesh for the first time. Though they had seen us they seemed but little frightened, and, cantering gently up the slope, disappeared over the crest. They were very handsome with their gray backs and white chests and legs.

Shortly after this we separated, Kermit going to the left and I to the right. Only a few moments after I left him I saw some animals among the rocks about 700 yards away. After studying them with the field-glasses, I found them to be six female poli with four young. Our first care was for the males, so we left them undisturbed, and hunted up a nullah to one side. We found nothing and worked our way back in the hope that some male poli had joined the females. None had, and, as we wished to hunt the country beyond, we walked toward them over a great snow-bank. They soon saw us and cantered gracefully away over the mountain. We then plodded through the deep snow to the crest of a saddle. Again we saw females but no males. We tramped along the ridges without success until dusk began to fall. Two native hunters were with us. They seemed to tire quicker than either Rahima or I, and at intervals protested that the hunting should end for the day. Just as the sun was setting we caught a glimpse of Kermit, who was following the same tactics with the same lack of success. He and his shikaries showed up as tiny black dots against the white of the opposite mountain crest. Night fell as it falls in the mountains, suddenly. The shadows lengthened, and we found ourselves in the cold darkness. Far across the valley white mountains still blazed in a golden light. Ten minutes more and night closed like an extinguisher over all. Kermit and I met in the valley and rode to camp together. As we passed the lakes, we heard from the black the querulous quacking of the ducks who had settled there again.

On the whole we were not discouraged by the day's work, for though we had seen no good heads, we had seen enough females and young to make us reasonably certain that there were some mature males near by. That evening, after talking with the natives in camp, we decided that the ravines we had hunted that day contained no mature rams and agreed to move to Subashi the next day. Accordingly, we sent a native forward that night to look the country over with a pair of our binoculars and to report when we arrived there.

We got to Subashi about one o'clock the following day. It was a valley with a little stream in the centre from which the land sloped up rather abruptly to surrounding hills. The ground was sandy, the vegetation sparse, but camels, sheep, and yaks seemed to be able to eke out a reasonable existence there. As it was evidently a place where there was no room for two separate guns, we decided to hunt together. Twice on our way up the valley we saw herds of female and young poli on the hillsides.

Soon we met the "jungli wallah" sent out the night before. He was in a state of great excitement. He told us that he had found a herd of eight goolja. We were delighted, and pushed forward cautiously to a point where the nullah forked. With our field-glasses we could just see them lying among some rocks toward the end of the right branch. The ravine, where the poli were, ended in some stiff-looking mountains. The left fork, slightly longer, ended near a divide beyond which lay the Russian Pamirs. Between the two branches was a high ridge of slide rock covered with snow.

Two stalks were possible, neither good; one over the top of the mountain on the extreme right, the other up the left nullah and over the dividing ridge. We chose the latter, for we were afraid we would not have time to complete the former. After riding a short way up the nullah, we left our horses and started climbing. As we approached the foot of the hill a very handsome red fox jumped up and trotted off. We wanted it for our collections, but did not shoot at it for fear of scaring off our poli. Somehow in hunting this very often happens. Smaller game always seems to show up during a stalk for big game.

The hill was a steep one. We zigzagged to and fro, floundering in snow and slipping on rock. The altitude was high, over 16,000 feet, and it cut our breath badly. At last, after an hour and a half of hard work, we reached the summit and peered over. To our sorrow we found that the poli, for some reason unknown to us, had moved and were slowly filing up a shoulder nearly 800 yards away. They were not really frightened, they were apprehensive. As it was now four-thirty, and there was no chance to try another stalk, we settled ourselves on the ridge for what Rahima called a "lookum see." Through the field-glasses and telescopes we could see the sheep plainly. They were very handsome as they stepped delicately along, now stooping to nibble a tuft of grass, now halting to glance around and sniff the wind. Occasionally one would clamber on a rock and stand sentinel-like, his head thrown back until the massive spiral horns seemed to rest upon his shoulders. Standing thus they looked like the very spirit of the mountains. We studied them carefully. They were eight in number. Six had horns about forty-five inches in length. Two were splendid animals with horns measuring fifty or better.

A knife-like wind had risen and we were getting the full force of it. To make the climb we had stripped off our heavy coats. We were soaked with sweat and were soon chilled through and through. Every one was shivering. It was hard to hold the telescope steadily enough to see the game. Kermit and I agreed that if we had had to shoot then, we would have been as likely to hit the moon as a poli. In spite of this, we stayed until almost dark in order to mark down where our game stopped.

Through the dusk we plodded down the hill. When we reached the foot, we saw down the valley the red glow of some yak-dung camp-fires. This at once explained the behavior of the rams. Our caravan had moved up to where the valley forked, and were in plain sight of the heights where the poli had been. Cold, weary, and rather disconsolate, we made our way to camp, determined to start again early next morning.

All night long the wind blew down the valley, singing and whistling around our camp. Our light canvas tent bellied in the wind, and time and again we thought it would blow over. The cold from the ground came right through our bedding-rolls. Toward midnight it began to snow, and fine powdery flakes whirled in on us. I had my shoes in bed with me to prevent them freezing stiff.

At 4.30 A. M. we got up. The snow had stopped, but the whole country was sheeted in white. We pulled on with numb fingers, the few clothes we had taken off, gulped down some coffee, and started up the nullah where we had last seen the animals. Soon day began to break. A cold, steely-gray sky, heavy with unshed snows, arched over us. We dismounted and walked, partly from caution, partly because it was too cold to ride even clothed as we were.

About six o'clock we saw our game. Unfortunately, one of the men had turned a bend of the ravine too quickly and they had glimpsed him. Again they were not frightened but only apprehensive, and they made off slowly across the end of the valley and up the steep slope of the mountain. We lay still and watched. At last they breasted the crest, showed for a moment outlined against the sky, and one by one disappeared on the other side.

As soon as they were out of sight we started to follow them. One of the Kirghiz was sent back with our yaks, while Kermit, Rahima, Khalil, a local hunter, and I tramped ahead. It was about half past six. At first the way was only moderately steep. Then it changed and we had to climb. We floundered through snow-drifts waist-deep on slopes where it was difficult to believe snow could rest. We climbed over shoulders of rock where the loose shale under its white covering made every step a slip.

The altitude rapidly increased, and soon we were at least 17,000 feet high. We snatched gasping at every mouthful of thin air. When we stopped to rest I threw myself flat, though Kermit only seemed to need to lean on his stick. About eight we reached the crest. Our hopes were high, for we felt from the way the poli were travelling they might be just the other side. Very cautiously we worked our way up to some jutting rocks and looked over. We saw nothing. By this time the sun was shining. After looking around for ten or fifteen minutes, the shikaries decided that they had gone beyond the next range, and suggested that we start down the slope. Fortunately, at this moment Kermit picked them up with the field-glasses. They were on the opposite side of the valley, perhaps a mile away, lying on a patch of snow. Had we gone down the slope, they surely would have seen us and run off.

With the wind as it was, only one stalk was possible. This entailed about five miles as the crow flies, during which we crossed two mountains and numerous spurs. The stalk began at once. We struggled across snow-banks many feet deep; we zigzagged over rock drifts; we stumbled through corries where the snow concealed deep holes between boulders into which we fell. We climbed hand over hand up rock shoulders. At one place Kermit and I tobogganed down a steep snow slope and nearly started a snowslide.

The sun on the snow had made a heavy mist that hung curtain-wise across the valley. At last we reached a little ravine flanked by a steep ridge from which we felt we would get a shot at our game. Up the slope we toiled, looking about for the poli. It was a hard task, for we had to snatch moments when gaps occurred in the mist as it rolled by before the wind. We had sweated heavily and our clothes were drenched. Now the knife-like wind cut us to the bone. More than six hours had passed while we were climbing. In the beginning I had consistently brought up the rear of the column, but toward the end, one of the shikaries and the "jungli wallahs" dropped behind me.

After watching carefully for about twenty minutes, we made sure the rams were not where we had last seen them. As Rahima put it, we were "very mad-going," for we had labored mightily on this

230

stalk. Suddenly the fog began to thin, shredded away, and we saw the sheep opposite us in the Russian Pamirs. They were perhaps 700 yards distant, but, as we were in plain sight on a snow-drift, we lay quite still. It looked as if we were doomed to "the long day's patience, belly down on frozen drift," when a cloud drifted up, and under cover of the dim light we were able to crawl cautiously out of sight. We started at once for a point nearer our quarry. The clouds began to bank over us in real earnest.

When we had reached a position somewhere between three or four hundred yards from the rams, we realized that a snow-storm, sweeping up the valley, would be on us in a very few minutes, and make shooting impossible. It was now or never. I had won the first shot, so settling myself very carefully in the snow I fired at the animal which seemed to me to present the best target. Kermit immediately followed suit. At the crack of the rifles the rams were up and away, but we thought our shots had hit. Fortunately they did not know where we were, and headed back in our general direction toward the Chinese Pamirs.

Running as hard as we could over the snow, we came to a point which would give us a clear view of them when they passed. I had snatched off my gloves to get a better grip on the rifle, and now my hands were so cold that I could not feel the trigger. Suddenly the sheep came into view from behind a huge buttress of rock. They were in single file, the big rams leading. They were about 250 yards away, going at a plunging canter through the drifts. Their great spiral horns flared out magnificently, their heads were held high. Every line was clear cut against the white of the snow.

We began firing at once at the two leaders. First one and then the other staggered and lost his place in the line. Though hard hit, they pulled themselves together, joined the herd, and all disappeared over a near-by ridge. Clutching our rifles, we stumbled after them. When we reached the trail we found blood-stains. We put every ounce of strength we had into the chase, for these were the trophies we had travelled 12,000 miles to get. The going was very bad. Every few steps we floundered arm-pit deep in the snow. It was like the foot-tied race of a nightmare. Try as we would, we could not make time. Suddenly the wind rose, snow began to drift down, and the trail was blotted out in the swirling white of the storm. We could do no more and had to give up and make for camp.

Working our way down to the valley we found our yaks, so frosted with snow that they looked like animated birthday-cakes. The two native hunters with them had seen the rams cross the ridge and were confident they were mortally wounded. They felt sure we would find them next day if the storm did not obliterate their trails. This was but poor comfort, as a blizzard was then raging, and even if we were lucky enough to find the sheep the wolves would have destroyed the body skins. From the sportsman's standpoint, of course, the great horns are the trophy, but for mounting in the museum the whole skin is necessary.

It was growing late. Thoroughly tired out we rode back through the storm to camp. The snow drifted in stinging particles against our faces. It was a moment when we fully appreciated the beards we had grown. Though far from ornamental they were a great protection. When we got to our tent they were stiff and heavy with snow and ice. After as hot a supper as we could get, we rolled up in our bedding. Storm or shine, we made up our minds to be off early next morning to the point where we had last seen our poli.

In the gray dawn we were up again. The storm had blown over during the night. Stars were glittering coldly over the white mountains. On our grunting yaks we plodded up the valley to the scene of yesterday's stalk. When we arrived the sun was just rising. Its rays, as they came through the mountain clefts, struck the snow slantwise and gave it a queer, unreal, coppery glow. The wind had blown much of last night's fall clear of the mountain slope in front of us. There we could see fragments of the poli trail which led up and over the crest.

The one thing to do was to follow the trail. Here

we struck an unexpected snag. Two of the three Kirghiz with us said that the slope ahead was too dangerous to climb, because we would almost certainly be caught in a snowslide. As these men had had a hard time the previous day, we felt that in this case their wish was father to their thought. Though the mountain looked steep and high, we insisted that the climb could be made.

Rahima Loon was really tired, so we left him with the yaks and began climbing. Our party consisted of Kermit, myself, Khalil, and three jungli wallahs, one of whom was as game as a bantam, while the other two were very sad. For four hours we plodded in zigzags up through the snow. It was back-breaking work. The trail had to be broken through drifts four to eight feet deep. The altitude was high, the air thin, and when at last we panted to the top we looked as if we had been in a Turkish bath.

On the other side of the ridge stretched a wide valley. It was seamed with rocky spurs from the surrounding mountains. The snow lay thick and undisturbed, for this side was sheltered from the wind which had swept the slope up which we had climbed. We could see no tracks, though we searched the country with our field-glasses for a long while. The animals might be lying dead behind any one of a thousand rocky shoulders, or be covered with snow.

The wind blew colder and colder. Even the Kirghiz huddled shivering in the lee of some rocks. Apparently the poli were hopelessly lost. Of the party, all shared our view but the cheerful "jungli wallah." He said he thought he stood a chance of finding them by circling back and up the valley into which we were looking. By so doing he could look up the ravines that ran down from the mountains. He said also that he hoped to mark them by wolf-tracks.

As there seemed little else to do we told him to go ahead, though we had but little faith in the result. Tramping down the slope again we reached camp in the late afternoon, very downhearted.

The "jungli wallah" followed out his plan. He went up the other valley, and, with some field-glasses we had lent him, studied the country. He saw seven wolves near the head of a small ravine and knew at once that one of our rams lay there. Going there he found not one, but two. The sheep had lain down close together after passing the ridge, and had died during the night. They were the two leaders and had fine heads. The horns of one measured fifty-one and a half inches, and the other forty-nine and a half. He brought them into camp late in the evening. We were delighted. They were our first poli and had good heads.

Though the wolves had served us well by making it possible for us to find our game, they had, as we feared, completely destroyed the body skins which made the rams of little value for exhibition purposes in the museum.

We had, of course, to get mountable specimens not only of adult males but of females and young males. If, however, we were not fortunate enough to get adult males with large heads, these big heads could be mounted on body skins of animals who were adult but whose horns were smaller.

There seemed to be no more poli in this nullah, so we decided to move our camp. We marched during the morning over the desolate plain which stretches south from the Little Kara Kul. To east of us towered Mustugh Ata in all the majesty of his 24,000 feet. Before us rose occasional flocks of gray snow-birds that flitted away like dead leaves before a November wind.

About noon we came to the village of Kara Su. Like the other Pamir villages which figure in bold type on the maps, it consists of four or five yourts. It lies at the foot of the valley of that name which leads, after four or five miles, over a low pass into the Russian Pamirs. Here the news we heard from the natives made us feel that this would be a good place to hunt. Moreover, the Russian Pamirs where we decided the poli would be were so close at hand that we were able to camp in the village. This had the real advantage of giving us a yourt to live in, which far outstrips a six-by-nine canvas tent as a winter residence in the Pamirs.

The inhabitants of Kara Su were very friendly. They came and squatted around our fire and nodded and smiled at us. We particularly liked one small boy. He was clothed in a single cotton wrapper-like garment. Just what its function was we could not decide. It certainly was not ornamental, for if dropped among the refuse by the yourt it could have been distinguished only with difficulty. It could not have been worn for warmth, as it was of the flimsiest material. Nor was it prescribed by modesty, for when standing by the fire the little fellow generally wound it around his neck and toasted his bare brown body before the coals. He was very friendly and cheerful, and much delighted by an empty tobacco tin and some colored buttons that we gave him.

As soon as we had made up our minds to camp at Kara Su, we left word for the caravan to stop at the yourts, and we started for the hunting-grounds. Our way up the valley of the Kara Su led through heavy sand and snow-drifts. The going was so bad and the altitude so high that the ponies we were riding were thoroughly blown, and we longed for yaks. At the end of about two hours we came to the pass, a low, sandy, wind-swept ridge. Beyond stretched rolling hills separated by barren valleys.

Almost immediately after we crossed the divide, one of the Kirghiz made out a herd of poli feeding on the dry grass-tufts in one of the bottoms. A short easy stalk brought us to a point above them on the hillside.

237

Something had alarmed them, and they were making off at a decorous canter across the valley. The herd was composed of young males and females. We wanted one or more of each for the museum so we fired, killing one and hitting two others. The herd broke into a gallop and disappeared. We trotted across the valley, and found that the animal we had killed was a young male. Leaving Khalil to skin him we started on the trail of the wounded. About a quarter of a mile farther we came to where another had broken off from the herd, and was lying down in a small ravine. I followed this animal, and Kermit went off on the remaining spoor.

When I got up to where the game was, I found it to be an adult female. Rahima was with me and together we skinned it. Here the balance of the party caught up with us, bringing the skin of the young male and the ponies. The first Kirghiz to arrive I sent off after Kermit with one of the horses. By the time we had finished it was dark and there was no sign of Kermit. I was worried, because to be benighted on the Pamirs at this time of year, in the intense cold, with the bitter storms that sweep them, is a very serious matter. The men were tired and far more philosophical as a result. "Kermit Sahib get back to camp, God give it," was their view of the situation. I explained that this placid attitude would not do, and organized search-parties. Taking our two shikaries with me, I sent out the Kirghiz who knew the country by themselves. In this latter disposition I made a mistake, for I found later that after letting a couple of whoops and getting no answer, they decided that their duty was done and returned to camp. The two shikaries and I rode up to the crest of the mountain and along it. Every few minutes we called but got no response. At last we found a trail through the snow leading back toward camp. We judged this was Kermit's and abandoned our search.

Arriving in camp at eight-thirty we found that Kermit had come in an hour earlier. It looked like waste effort, but in early winter in the Pamirs it does not pay to take a chance.

Next morning at three o'clock we were up and off again. Both of us were shivering cold in spite of wearing nearly everything we had. I felt much like the man in "The Hunting of the Snark," who wore seven coats and three pair of boots. We had changed our ponies for yaks, which made us much more comfortable. Work such as we had had the day before would have been play to a yak.

Before dawn we were on the hunting-grounds and had selected a point of vantage. There we waited huddled up in our coats, while black turned to gray, gray to pink, and the first rays of sunlight struck across the hills. Through our glasses we picked up herds of females in several places, but no adult males. Two or three times we thought we saw rams, but each time a close scrutiny proved that we had been mistaken. We changed our position a half a dozen times without result. Once we did see two small rams trotting over a hill-crest, but though we followed them we could not find where they went.

At last about noon we made out in a valley a large herd of females, and near them four rams. After studying the latter our men said they had heads measuring forty inches or better. We could see that they were adults. They were strolling leisurely along the slope toward the head of a ravine. As usual the wind was wrong, and we had to make a long détour to head them off. By the time we had done so, and reached the point where we had planned to intercept them, they had disappeared. Though we looked as carefully as we could, we could find no sign of them. Also the snow was too much marked with trails, old and new, to help us. We held a council of war and decided that the sheep must have gone up the ravine.

We made another détour, and climbed the ridge again. Our judgment proved correct, for here Khalil picked up the sheep lying among some rocks still farther toward the head of the valley. Again we climbed through the snow and rock for a mile or so. Crossing the ridge, we worked down a little rocky shoulder just above where we believed the poli were lying. We could not see them and thought they had moved again. We started down the ridge. Suddenly one of the native Kirghiz, who was with Kermit on the left, called out that he saw them.

There was no time to lose for the sheep had seen us and were running. Kermit started shooting at once and, as I came running up, dropped one. A few seconds later I hit another who rolled down the steep slope like an enormous rabbit. We knocked over a third, but he picked himself up again and went off.

We scrambled down the steep hillside, and found to our disappointment that the horns of Kermit's animal were just short of forty inches, and mine still smaller. They were, however, adults in body, and the skins could be used by the museum for mounting the two large heads.

Kermit went with Khalil to look for the trail of the wounded ram. Rahima and I started to measure and skin the two dead animals. While we were doing so a Kirghiz man, a little Kirghiz boy, and a very large yellow dog came up and joined us. Forgetting that they were Mohammedans, and that the meat was unclean because the animals had not been "hallaled" before death, I told them they could have some. Here in the back mountains where food is scarce, religious precepts were not so strict. They solemnly cut the throats of the long-dead carcass and sawed off great chunks of meat, which they carried away.

By the time we were well started on our work, the yaks came plodding solemnly over the hillside, led by the man with whom we had left them. Many hands proverbially make light work. With his help we had the skins off and the trophies slung over the yaks, when Kermit and Khalil came back to say that the blood-trail of the wounded ram had been lost in a corrie of rocks.

The sky had become cloudy and overcast. The forbidding gray of an approaching snow-storm arched over us. The natives had been hurrying as rapidly as they could, casting apprehensive glances at the gathering clouds. We mounted and started for camp.

A short distance up the valley a debate took place between the two Kirghiz. One wished to go back the way we came. The other wanted to take a short cut over a mountain and try to get to camp before the storm broke. The latter triumphed and we started to zigzag up a steep slope. Every hundred yards the snow became deeper, until when we reached the top it was up to the bellies of the yaks. At just this moment the storm broke on us like a blizzard on the Montana plains.

The wind shrieked by with such force that we could lean against it. The snow whirled down in blinding clouds. It penetrated every crack and cranny of our clothes. I could just make out Kermit's yak a few yards in front of me. One of the Kirghiz dismounted and stumbled ahead on foot. Even these natives lost their bearings. We plunged through banks of snow and over concealed boulders. The

242

great yaks, white-crusted until they looked like moving snow-drifts, plodded sturdily along. They crossed obstacles with the even calm of caterpillar-tractors. Once we saw huddled under the lee of a rock some ramchukor, the snow drifting in eddies around them. At last after an hour's work, we suddenly found ourselves on the brink of a steep slope. The Kirghiz recognized it. Down it we slipped and slid to the comparative shelter of the valley. In another hour we were back at our yourt.

We had our sportsman's trophies, the two big heads. We had our group of poli for the museum. The essential part of our work with the poli was done. We stood around the small fire in the yourt, the melting ice and snow dripping from our beards and clothes. Rahima, who had a healthy respect for winter in the Pamirs and passes of the Himalayas, summed up his views by saying:

"All right, good morning, going!"

CHAPTER X

ACROSS THE WINTRY HIMALAYAN PASSES BACK TO KASHMIR

LEAVING Karasu, we marched through a barren and desolate countryside to Tagharma, in the Sarikol Pamirs. One feels that it is a very old land, but there is little tangible evidence of its antiquity. The mud-daubed stone houses of the villages are probably the counterparts of those that stood here two thousand years ago; no doubt many of the rocks used in the buildings are identical, but there is nothing to tell one so. Everything of man's handiwork has taken on the ageless dun hue of the desert. On some big boulders near where we made our noonday halt, there were scratched rough likenesses of the ovis poli.

Tagharma might claim title as an oasis because of the presence of a few straggling willow-trees. Here the Rajah of Sarikol came to meet us, a pleasant-appearing boy clad in a tunic of purple plush. His retainers were a fierce-eyed, hawk-featured set; totally unlike our Kirghiz friends in bearing and physique. Some travellers credit this obvious Aryan race to Alexander the Great's expeditionary force, which must have been marvellously prolific if all the isolated Aryan tribes found throughout this part of the Himalayas are really from remnants of that army.

Next morning we rode in to Tashkurghan, running the gauntlet of a series of refreshment booths set out for us by hospitable Beys. Rustum Bey was the first to halt us and escort us into the dried mud shelter in which he had spread carpets for our reception. Here we drank the inevitable tea of ceremony from the grimy china bowls, and ate a few nuts and watermelon seeds. We had already taken an early tiffin in order to leave us free to start immediately on our bundo-bust when we should arrive at Tashkurghan, so at each additional gathering we dreaded still further the drinking and eating which the acceptance of the courtesy would call for.

Last of all out rode the Amban, and of a truth "the nightmare Life in Death was he." It seemed impossible that he could sit upon his horse unsupported, so emaciated was he. His skin was drawn tight over his features, like old yellow parchment. The guard that accompanied him was the most motley troop that I have ever in my wanderings come across. In comparison with it, the raggedest group of South American insurrectos would have appeared like a battalion of West Point cadets.

Tashkurghan has had a long and eventful history, but little remains to show for it. It is mentioned in Ptolemy's "Geography," and way before the days of Marco Polo it was a centre where the trade from the Far East met that of Persia. The ruins of the ancient stone fort (Tash—stone, kurghan—fort) can

still be traced; the Amban inhabits the modern one.
Probably most of the material in the new fort was
originally used in the old. The bazaar is a single
street a hundred yards long, boasting perhaps six
shops. The sentiments of Thangbrand, Olaf's priest,
kept running through my mind, but, profiting by his
difficulties, I did not say:

> "What's the use
> Of this boasting up and down,
> When three women and a goose
> Make a market in your town?"

The old gray-bearded Aksakal quartered us in his
house, which stood in what was the most extensive
and attractive garden in town—there were four small
trees in it. Tashkurghan is Nadir Beg's home, and
he brought to see us his small son, an attractive alert
boy of eight. The Aksakal had six or seven children,
one of whom, a round-eyed youngster of some four
summers, was quite evidently his favorite. He was
a solemn little fellow, and took deep interest in everything that we did, following us about with great dignity. We gave him a store of treasures in the shape
of large red and green buttons, empty tobacco tins,
and other odds and ends.

We had decided that Tashkurghan would be the
best place at which to make the final cuts in our
equipment before starting back across the passes to
Kashmir. Of necessity, having no idea how long we

would have to spend in the Pamirs after ovis poli, we had brought with us from Kashgar a certain amount of surplus equipment. Now that we had secured the group of the great sheep, we determined to put in only two more hunting days. If fortune favored us and we got a couple more rams, so much the better, but our followers seemed so apprehensive of the snow-covered passes ahead that we did not feel justified in spending much additional time on the Pamirs.

The process of cutting down was not accomplished without considerable effort. The Oriental has strongly embedded in him the habit of acquisition. If you throw anything away, it is ten to one that some one of your servants will salvage it, no matter how utterly useless it may be. Thus you will find that your endeavor to lighten loads has merely meant a redistribution. Ted and I finally adopted the principle of presenting anything that we no longer required, and which we knew could be of no service to our men, to some needy or deserving native. Vigilance could not invariably be relaxed even then, for the gift might be requisitioned from its new owner.

The time had come when we no longer needed the evening clothes which had served us so well for our ceremonial calls upon the Ambans of Turkestan. Nadir Beg fell heir to mine, but Ted's was kept and presented to a follower of the Mir of Hunza, who made himself particularly useful to us.

Occasionally we hid our lesser belongings as a sort of Easter-egg hunt for the inhabitants of some village where we had spent the night. In this way I concealed in the felt lining of a yourt in which we had slept an old pair of cotton pajamas. It so happened, however, that the yourt was dismantled upon our departure, and we had not gone many miles before a Sarikuli came galloping after us, waving the discarded pajamas. Still, in one way or another, our efforts were crowned with success, for when we started down the Hunza we had only twelve pony-loads all told, and among them were comprised six ovis poli skins and eight heads.

After much consultation Rahima advised Payik Nullah as the most profitable place to put in our last days after poli. The new caravan which we had engaged in Kashgar had proved to be far and away the least efficient of any of the caravans we had had. They were hopelessly dilatory in getting under weigh in the mornings, and marched at a snail's pace when once they did get going. We hoped that by making good marches and letting them come in after dark, we could give them a practical lesson in the advantages of early starting and steady marching. We explained this principle to them on the first evening on which they came in, complaining and groaning, in the cold and dark, but they were apparently hopelessly shiftless, and unable to profit by even the most practical illustrations.

We determined, therefore, to give our slow-moving caravan the advantage of the last days' hunting, and by sending it on ahead we hoped that it would reach Misgar before us. We were most fortunate in having the very efficient Nadir Beg with us, for in putting him in charge of this advance caravan, we knew that it would be capably managed.

The first night out from Tashkurghan we halted at Jurgal Gumbaz, and on the second at Jayloo, where we found a most welcome stone hut in which we waited snugly for the shiftless caravan, instead of shivering under the shelter of a rock, as we had anticipated.

A couple of hours' marching next morning brought us to Payik Karaul, and here, with a few horses bearing our bedding and food, we left the main road. We followed up Payik Nullah for some fifteen miles, until we came to where the yourts of Daoud Beg were pitched. He had come to Tashkurghan to meet us, and his nephew Palang was reputed, and rightly so, to be the best shikarry around. We had brought no tent, but a roomy yourt in which a fire of yak dung burned proved far superior to any tent. Daoud Beg's numerous offspring crowded in to look the strangers over, and on them we bestowed the gaudy buttons which we always carried in our pockets to serve on such occasions.

Before daylight next morning Loosu brought us in the two cups of tea that form chota hazri (little breakfast) and, inspirited by them, we reluctantly crawled out of our warm bedding-rolls. Our saddles had been put on yaks, for we had some steep and rocky climbing ahead of us. The shaggy coats of the yaks were white with hoarfrost, as we clambered stiffly into our saddles. Our path lay over a steep pass, on the farther side of which we found ourselves in the Russian Pamirs. By this time the sun was up, and, although we were still most grateful for our heavy leathern coats with their sheepskin lining, we felt less the necessity for concentrating our thoughts entirely upon keeping warm, and were able to give some attention to the neighboring mountainsides. The first thing we saw was a big red fox homeward bound from his night's rambles, and shortly afterward Palang made out a herd of arkal or ovis poli ewes. It was not until after we had seen still another lot of ewes that Khalil picked up two rams. One was standing and the other lay stretched out on the rubble. We could see that the former had a fine head; that of the latter was only partly visible, and did not look as good. The wind, of course, was wrong, which, together with the conformation of the country, called for a long and roundabout stalk. We were able, however, to go the greater part of the way on our yaks. Bos Grunniens has been well named; he grunts and pants like an asthmatic patriarch as he climbs, but he plods along regardless, and the minute you stop him he starts eating snow, or boortsa, if there be any about. Before we came to the last rise dividing us from our quarry, a fox jumped up and trotted across ahead of us. We feared it would move the poli, and either it or something else did, for when we had reached the vantage-point from which they should have been visible and within range, they were nowhere to be seen.

Cautiously we examined the country roundabout, but they had evidently gone some distance, so we kept on along the ridge, making numerous halts to spy out the land. We came upon a herd of females and young, and watched them through our field-glasses as they pursued their noonday occupation of feeding and sleeping. We had a little cold mutton and bread with us, and while we were eating it, sheltered as well as possible from the bitterly cold wind that whipped across the ridge, Palang went ahead, scouting on his own. Half an hour later he appeared on a ridge, waving to us to join him. We were not long in reaching him, and he explained with whisper and gesture that he had seen the rams lying down below some big rocks.

It was necessary to proceed very carefully and slowly, for, although the wind for once favored us, the slide rock was treacherous and a rolling stone would quickly put the poli on the alert and probably send them off at the double. Step by step we picked our way among the boulders. We came to where Palang had seen the rams, and, peeping over, we caught a glimpse of the head of one of them. He seemed to be standing up, but drowsing on his feet. Ducking back, we continued along the ridge to a heap of rocks we had marked down as the end of our stalk. We reached it in safety, and, peering over, saw a fine poli ram only seventy-five yards away. Ted had won the toss for first shot. As soon as I heard the report of his rifle, I also let drive, quickly reloading in case the second ram should show up. Ted had fired his second shot at his ram, when the other poli popped into sight; I quickly let drive, and after that the shooting became general. We each fired four times, and each bullet scored a hit. I was able to get several snap-shots of one of the wounded animals. They were fine big fellows; Ted's had a fifty-three-inch horn and mine a fifty-two.

We were eager to secure another female for the museum group, so after a last congratulatory look at our prizes, we left Rahima and Khalil to take the skins off while we faced the main ridge again with Palang. It was a stiff climb, and when we had made the ascent we found that the ewes upon which we had designs had decamped. Climbing or even walking on the level at these high altitudes involves much more labor than can be imagined by those who have not experienced it. In Persian this region is called the Bam-i-Dunya, the Roof of the World, and from this is, I suppose, derived the name Pamirs, for "B" and "P" are easily interchangeable. It is indeed a roof, and a high one; we were often hunting at an altitude of 17,000 feet.

Palang was both indefatigable and cheerful, so on we went in search of the ewes, but it was almost too dark to shoot before we came upon a bunch. There was no chance for a stalk, so we chanced a few long-range shots without success. It was a stiff pull back to camp; there was no moon, but the white of the snow gave some light, and the stars shone out in glittering brilliancy. Daoud Beg had sent out two ponies, but we were glad to change back to our yaks for the final descent from the pass. The dark and the hidden stones bothered the yaks not a bit; the steepest and most uncertain short cut only incited them to additional speed when they were headed down-hill. However, you soon acquired a blind and unreasoning confidence in their ability to keep their feet under any circumstances. On the steep slopes the snow lay in strips and patches that shone with a phosphorescent glow in the dark. In spite of the bitter cold we could find thought to thoroughly enjoy the wild scene, doubly so with the knowledge of the two fine poli that our shikaries had brought in ahead of us. It was nearly half past eight before we were thawing ourselves out at the welcome yak-dung fire in our yourt.

We had still one day more that we felt justified in allotting to ourselves for hunting, and we determined to make a last try for the extra ewe that we wanted. In the morning, therefore, we sent our two shikaries down to Payik Karaul with the pack-ponies, while we took Palang and a couple of other local shikaries and went off to Gunjabat Nullah, reputed a most likely ground. Riding up the ravine we came upon both sheep and ibex heads, all old and weather-beaten. The first game we saw was a large herd of ibex; we watched them through our glasses, and estimated two of the large males as having horns at least forty-five inches in length, a very good size for the Himalayan ibex. It was not, however, ibex that we wanted, so we continued our search. It was only a few minutes later that we made out four poli rams. They looked larger than any one we had yet seen, so we immediately set out upon a lengthy and toilsome stalk which if successful should bring us within good range. For four hours we struggled along through deep snow and slide rock. Palang was most distrustful of avalanches—he had lost four friends in one—and we did our best to avoid setting anything in motion. The only restful part of the stalk was when we tobogganned down a steep bit of mountainside in the track of an avalanche. It would have been better fun had we not realized that for every foot we gaily coasted we would have to elsewhere plod upward a corresponding distance. Several immature avalanches came down, while the two shikaries and I were making our way along the foot of the hill, and I did not pay much attention to them. Of a sudden I heard them shout, and looked up to see Ted humming down in the middle of a small avalanche. For-

tunately he was able to keep on the surface, so that
when the snow slowed up he extricated himself without having suffered any damage.

It was tedious work winning our way up to the
ridge from which we hoped to make the tag end of
the stalk, and disappointment was awaiting us at the
top; the sheep were no longer there. The man who
had stayed behind with the yaks, and who had been
instructed to watch the rams, told us that they appeared to get our wind when we were about half
through the stalk, and that by the time we appeared
on the crest they had been gone for two hours! Whatever it was that disturbed them, it had done its work
thoroughly, for the poli had left the country at a
round trot, and put a good day's march between us
and themselves. During the rest of the day we saw
nothing but a herd of female ibex, so empty-handed
we worked our way back to the main nullah and
headed down to Payik Karaul. For the latter part of
the ride Ted and I shifted back to ponies. Work as
hard as we could, it seemed impossible for us to keep
our yaks going at any reasonable pace, except when
they were bound down-hill. The Sarikulis could keep
them going apparently without effort. Our escort,
which consisted of three men, also changed mounts;
one climbed on to a huge camel, another got on a
pony, and the third shifted to a fresh yak. As they
rode along, all three abreast, ahead of us, we could
only regret that it was too dark to use the camera.

There are two passes from the Pamirs over into the Hunza Valley—the Mintaka and the Killik. The former offers the more direct route, but is much more difficult to negotiate in bad weather. Our Sarikuli friends insisted upon taking us over the Killik, assuring us that by so doing we would reach Misgar sooner than if we went the shorter way. We marched from Payik Karaul to a group of yourts known as Khush Bel; it was well over thirty miles and our Kashgar caravan men ran true to form in getting off late, so that it was not until after nine that they came in—a frozen and woebegone lot.

On the way we met the mail runner that comes through once a week from Gilgit to Kashgar. The fact that he had chosen the Killik impelled us to put more faith in the selection of our Sarikulis. This mail is run through in relays, and takes about a month to get from Srinagar to Kashgar. The runner told us he had seen poli rams near Khush Bel. Of course they had decamped by the time we reached there, but not far from the yourts we came upon the skulls of several big rams; they had been killed by wolves when the snow lay deep and the weight of their great horns wore them down when they tried to run from their foes. It must have been several years ago, for there was one head just short of sixty inches that I would have liked to have taken along had it not been so weather-worn as to make it useless. We had been continually on the lookout for good pick-ups, but this was the only one that we came on which was larger than those we shot.

At Khush Bel we were lodged in a yourt for the last time; we saw none after we had crossed the Killik. On the Pamirs we noted one reversal of nature as we had hitherto found it. The cats were most friendly and came up to be stroked and petted, while the dogs were unchangeably savage, and showed no inclination to be conciliated. There were only a few cats, but they were fine large fellows; one tried to get into my bedding-roll with me on a particularly cold night.

We crossed the Killik under favorable conditions; the ascent was long but gradual; the altitude was only 15,600, which seemed low after the great heights which we had topped between Leh and Yarkand. On the way over it came on to snow, but when we started to descend, it was not long before we left the snow behind.

The country for some time was unbelievably barren and desolate. We had heard a place mentioned, Shirin Maidan, the translation being the Polo Field. On reaching it we were disappointed to find it was merely a small plateau a couple of hundred yards long and half as wide, the only level spot of that size for miles around. The larger of the stones had been dragged off and ranged on either side. The Hunza men are very keen on polo, but as far as we could see, the only time when they could use this field would be on their way across the pass.

Our halt was to be Mukurshi, the junction of the Killik and Mintaka River, and a few miles before we reached it we quite unexpectedly began to come upon small bushes and even trees—willows and stunted cedars. Our two Sarikulis were mounted on yaks. They were riding along in the lead, except for Rahima, who had left his pony and walked on ahead. The trail was very steep and winding. Rahima sat down beside it to wait for us just where it made a sharp turn. As the leading yak pushed his head around the bend, he caught sight of Rahima and took fright. I heard his snort, and saw him plunge off the trail down the all but perpendicular mountainside. It seemed as if nothing could save him or his rider; a pony could not have kept his footing for an instant, but would have rolled over to be dashed to pieces long before he struck the stream below. By some miraculous process known only to yaks, the beast did keep his feet, and, after plunging down a short way, straightened himself out and slanted across the face of the mountain to reach the trail a little way on. Neither yak nor rider seemed in any degree flustered.

Mukurshi we found uninhabited, but there were many willow-trees growing in the small delta between the two streams, and plenty of dead branches with which we made a roaring fire, a fine contrast to the less spectacular but by no means to be despised fires of yak dung to which we had been confined during our hunting on the "world's white roof-tree."

Next day saw us at Misgar, a tiny village where we once more made the acquaintance of telegraph-poles, that invariable harbinger of civilization. There were a couple of lonely telegraph operators, exiled for a year to this far-flung outpost. At Misgar we sent back our Kashgar caravan. It was the first caravan from which we had parted without regret. Its members had been thoroughly incompetent without any disarming or redeeming features.

All down the Hunza gorge we used mixed caravans, a few ponies, a donkey or two, and the balance in porters. The entire outfit was generally changed twice a day, and as we got lower down the valley we changed more often. The worst day we had in this respect was on the march between Minapin and Chalt, only about fifteen miles, but calling for six shifts. When we swapped transport at a village there was never much delay, and the porters swung along at a round gait which put them at their journey's end in jig-time. The longest march we made was of twenty-six miles; but we kept up a good average, for with winter coming on we had no desire to delay in reaching the passes over into Kashmir. On the fifteen-mile stretch which I have mentioned, the multiplicity of shifts was further complicated by the fact that they took place at the most inconvenient places. Often the village where the coolies lived was some distance off up the mountainside. The men who had finished their turn would squat beside the loads and start upon a series of catcalls to summon their successors from hut and field. We needed a lot of small change to effect payment, for the coolies on the shorter hauls drew only an anna—about two cents—apiece. The Hunza men we found to be marked individualists; they rarely travelled in a long, sheep-like column. Usually they hove up in the early morning, shouldered their loads, and set off in groups of ones and twos. They were a cheerful, uncomplaining set of men.

In spite of its cumbersome size, I had toted with me my old copy of Knight's "Where Three Empires Meet," and the anticipated pleasure of rereading it while passing through the country about which so much of it had been written, more than repaid me for the space it had taken in the yakdan. It is unfortunately very rarely that books of travel and adventure are well enough written to hold the attention of any save those who are intimately acquainted with or deeply interested in the country with which they deal. Knight's books have ever proved such a happy exception; and I have followed him to many parts of the world since my mother first gave me the "Voyage of the Falcon." Among the Himalayan hunting-books my personal favorite remains Major Kennion's "Sport in the Further Himalayas." Rahima Loon in his younger days hunted with Kennion and had many a tale to tell of the remarkable stalks that the Major had made.

Between Misgar and Gilgit we passed through the

countries ruled by the Mirs of Hunza and of Nagar. The account of the campaign in which they were brought to realize the advisability of allowing subjects of the British Raj to pass unharmed through their dominions is vividly told by Knight. Both rulers claim descent from Alexander the Great through a mountain spirit that Alexander is supposed to have met on the Hindu Koosh. The Hunza branch of the family is very European in feature; all of its members with whom we came in contact were red-headed. The present Mir dyes his red hair black, but his sons leave it its natural hue.

We noticed a good deal of change in the color and profiles of the inhabitants as we came on down the valley. In the upper part the men were whiter in color and more aquiline in feature than were those lower down. The Mir of Hunza's subjects are usually known as Kanjutis, and the upper reaches of the Hunza River below the junction of the Killik and Mintaka streams is called the Kanjut River.

At Gircha, a short day's march below Misgar, we were met by the Mir. His travelling orchestra came out to escort us into town. It was led by an old greybeard playing an abbreviated trumpet. There were two other trumpets, two kettledrums, and two large drums. On one side of the latter the drummer beat with his hand and on the other side with a stick.

The Mir is a fine-looking man and a pleasant companion. He speaks Hindustanee, so we could dispense with interpreters. He was on his way up to a favorite hunting nullah, and had with him three or four hawks which he used on chukor. He tried a few shots with my Springfield rifle and made excellent practice.

That evening we dined in state with him, and an excellent dinner we had, for although I have never known Rousslia's superior as a Safari cook, still a change, when not for the worse, is always agreeable.

We had now cut down our equipment to the extent that we had only the clothes we stood in. The tuxedos which had served us so faithfully at many an Amban's feast we had given away as baksheesh. The Mir presented each of us with a Hunza choga, a long, loose sort of wrapper; Ted's was made from goat hair and embroidered with silk, mine was woven from ibex hair but unembroidered. These we slipped on over our worn hunting-clothes, and felt greatly bettered in appearance.

After dinner we adjourned to the garden to see some Kanjuti dances. There were various kinds, ranging from a slow and stately affair in which several men recited in Persian as they danced, to a wild performance where two men rushed about whirling their swords, and slashing the air so close to each other's heads that it was a miracle that no ears parted company with their owners. The whole scene was lighted by a roaring bonfire; beside it were ranged the men who beat their tomtoms in accompaniment to the performers, and massed behind them were the wild-featured tribesmen. It was a savage picture lit by the flickering tongues of flame one instant, and the next only half discerned in the darkness. Now one of the swordsmen was rushing about the circle in feigned flight, closely followed by his victorious antagonist. The excitement mounted like strong wine to the heads of the spectators, and they shouted mad encouragement. It was easy to see that we were among a warlike people, who until recently had made the greater part of their livelihood through raiding the Leh and Yarkand caravans, and carrying off and selling as slaves such members of the neighboring tribes as they could overpower or capture by stealth.

Their warlike valor may be gauged by the fact that in the short campaign against them in which Knight took part, out of the handful of British officers engaged therein, no less than three won the coveted Victoria Cross.

Since leaving the Tian Shan we had passed through various seasons. Before coming over the Muzart Pass we had been in late autumn, in Turkestan we had found ourselves in late summer, and then in early fall. In the Pamirs it had been bleak winter, but now as we dropped farther down the Kanjut Valley we were once more in the fall of the year. The colors were particularly beautiful against the barren background of the sterile mountains. The maple and poplar leaves were yellow, and the apricot-trees were red; a few of the walnuts were still green. At first the oases were small, but they steadily increased in size; some, the larger, showed a perfect wealth of color, reminding us of fall days on Long Island, with the dogwood in full glory. We often watched the goatherds shaking a golden rain of leaves from the trees, while their flocks waited expectantly beneath to browse upon them.

The Kanjutis are far from rich; they lead a hand-to-mouth existence, and during the summer months some villages subsist entirely on ripe fruit. The wolf is never far from the door, even at the best of times, and one of the reasons why there are so few foreigners allowed in the Hunza country is that the use of the natives as porters takes them from their work in the fields, and still further limits the grain supply. Of course, there aren't very many porters available, anyway.

The trail down the valley we found in excellent shape; the worst going we encountered was where it crossed the Batura glacier, and there for two or three miles it was hard work for the coolies and ponies.

At Gulmit the Mir has a house where he spends a couple of months each fall, and here we met his eldest son. We had passed another brother near Mukurshi. He was on his way to visit a wife who for some reason chose to live near Tashkurghan. With the Mir there was a third grown son and a small boy of five, a pretty dark-eyed little fellow, quite evidently the Benjamin of the family, for the Mir kept the child always beside

him, and was obviously very proud of him. Old
Daoud Beg at Payik and the graybeard Aksakal of
Tashkurghan also had Benjamins. It seemed a common trait among these people to favor the child of
their advanced years above his elder brothers and sisters. When we asked the Mir how many sons he had—
in enumerating their progeny our friends here never
counted in their girl children—he threw up his hands
and said it was really impossible for him to say. In
a fairly literal sense he is reputed to be the father
of his country. I may add, however, that the sons
whom we met all did him credit.

The capital of the kingdom is Baltit, the centre of
a group of villages collectively known as Hunza. The
Royal Palace overlooks the whole from the eminence
of a small hill. It is a roomy, rambling patchwork
Eastern affair, with no pretension to architecture of
any sort. Below it fell tier after tier of terraced field
and orchard. Deep lanes lined with high stone walls
wove an intricate pattern through the whole. On the
tops of some of the low stone houses heaps of golden
red corn were lying, adding a glorious splash of color
to the already brilliant effect of the turning leaves.
The Kanjuti likes color, and many of them we passed
on the road had yellow or red chrysanthemums stuck
in their caps. As a whole, they seemed a cheerful lot,
ever ready with a pleasant smile and a salaam. Many
of them struck us as being easy to mistake for Italians, and, curiously enough, their language sounded

much like Italian. In saying this, I hasten to add that I am not trying to suggest any kinship between the two peoples.

We rode on through Baltit and crossed the river over into the domains of the Mir of Nagar, spending the night at an attractive little town, Minapin. We were right beneath mighty Rakaposhi, towering above us with its altitude of 25,550 feet. Ten days before a terrific wind-storm had rushed down from its rugged slopes, cutting a swathe 400 yards wide through the edge of Minapin, but biting more deeply into the adjoining hamlet of Pisan. Two men, four horses, and many goats were killed, but more fatal than any loss of life had been the damage done to the fruit-trees, mercilessly mowed down in scores before the storm. Their loss meant that next summer starvation would stare the villages in the face.

Bird life was abundant in the lower valley. At Mukurshi we had seen only a few finches, but near Misgar we met an old friend whom we had first seen in the Sind Valley, a lovely little water-bird, with a black head, white waistcoat, and red coat and tail. We came across our first magpie sitting on an ice rock in the middle of the Batura glacier, with not another live thing for miles around. Lower down magpies became very common, flitting about on every side, uttering their rusty chatter. Our best friends were the pigeons, but I doubt if they reciprocated the feeling, for many was the good meal we made from roasted pigeon.

Chukor also helped supply the deficiencies of our larder. We had with us an old three-barrelled gun. At first it had a tendency to explode the shells whenever you snapped the breech shut. Cherrie set about remedying this, and was so successful that the gun would not go off even when you wished it to. Then the local gunsmiths in the larger towns where we halted tried a hand at it. After that it was "regularly irregular," as Ted put it. Sometimes both barrels could be fired, sometimes one, sometimes none. At last it got so that Khalil was the only person who could coax a shot out of it, and for some weeks he alone used it. After Gilgit a rapid disintegration set in, and even Khalil had to abandon it.

We reached Gilgit on October 30, having come down from Misgar in seven days. Major Loch, the Political Agent,—Administrator of Native Affairs,— put us up at his most comfortable house, loaned us his clothes to enable us to appear a little less disreputable, and did everything to help us through to Kashmir. I think that what we appreciated most of all was the delicious ale with which he greeted us on our arrival. We objected only as much as bare politeness and our knowledge of the difficulty with which all transport reached Gilgit dictated, when he insisted in giving us some more for the trip down.

The little willow-shaded European graveyard at Gilgit is a résumé of what life on the far Asian frontier means. Among the few graves there were that of

Hayward the explorer, murdered by the tribesmen, one of a young officer who had fallen over a precipice when hunting ibex, one of another officer killed in a punitive expedition in the mountains, still another of a political agent who had died of enteric. Last there was the pitiful little grave of a baby still born, with the mother so far from all comfort and assistance.

In front of Major Loch's house stands a large cannon that was brought back after the capture of Baltit in 1893. The story runs that a Chinaman from Yarkand told the then Mir that he could cast him a cannon larger than that owned by any of his neighbors. The Mir accordingly confiscated all the metal pots and pans in his capital, and from them the cannon was cast. The Mir next prudently insured that none of his neighbors should possess a larger one by cutting off the Chinaman's head. The piece was certainly a triumph when the rough facilities the maker had to hand are considered. It is far superior to several smaller pieces that stood near it. Major Loch told us that one of his predecessors had taken it out and used it on a punitive expedition against some of the nearby tribesmen.

We left Gilgit on October 31, and marched thirty-five miles to Bunji. The next day took us through what used to be the village of Ramghat, but a year ago a great rock avalanche swept down and levelled the greater part of the houses. Our march had taken us down the Gilgit River to where it empties into the

Indus; it is here that the great bend of the Indus occurs, and this Haramosh country harbors on its wild, barren mountains the best markhor. It was tantalizing to be so near and yet be forced to hurry past. We soon left the Indus and turned off up the Astore River, which we would follow now until we came to the dreaded Burzil Pass.

At the little village of Astore we saw the solitary grave of Lieutenant Davison, who had taken part with Knight in the Hunza campaign.

Ted and I still had with us our faithful riding ponies that we had brought from the Tian Shan. We had spared them wherever possible, but they were fairly fagged, so we walked the greater part of each day's march. We were so hard by now that a fifteen-mile trek did no more than give us a good appetite!

In the Astore Valley we were once more in the land of trees; that is to say, what might be called wild trees, in contradistinction to those that could grow only where man had through irrigation builded an oasis. It was sad in the deserted oases to see the trees standing gaunt and bare and dead. Now, for the first time since leaving the Tian Shan, the hillsides were covered with evergreens—tall pines and gnarled cedars. The smell of the cedar berries at one leap took me back to childhood days in the Fairy Apple Orchard of Sagamore.

On November 5 we faced the Burzil Pass. The

desire to remain where it lay. However, we were getting down; we had passed a pill-box house built up on stilts twenty-five feet above the ground. This was a landmark to the men. They explained that the snowdrifts piled up level with its floor. A mile or so on, to our surprise, we came upon a few lightly laden ponies attempting to get over to Sardar Chauki. One of the trail-breakers glanced at me out of the tail of his eye and began groaning and humping his back; as we reached the oncoming ponies he threw himself down beside the trail in a dismal heap. It was really wasted histrionics, for on seeing the approaching caravan we had decided that we might as well send our six voorloopers back with it. Upon being told of this the sick man made a most rapid recovery. They were all afraid that the pass would now be closed for many days.

We now had an easy trail to follow and made the rest of the distance without trouble. At the Dak Bungalow of Burzil Chauki we stopped at half past five and made a cup of tea. We had breakfasted at five in the morning, so we were very hungry. Then we pushed on down the valley another five miles to Minamarg, completing a twenty-four-mile march, with every one in excellent spirits at having the Burzil Pass behind us.

It was snowing hard next morning, and though we could look back toward the Burzil with satisfaction, we could not but feel a certain apprehension about the Raj-diangan. We rode down along a rushing stream, with steep hills rising on either hand. Sometimes the trail wound through fine forests; elsewhere there were open grass-covered stretches. Sheltering beneath the tufts of grass were myriads of finches; as they rose it seemed as if the hillside had in some miraculous fashion started to life.

Two easy marches took us to the foot of the Raj-diangan Pass over to Tragbal. This was the last barrier that separated us from Kashmir, and the Weather Gods were kind. A brilliant frosty morning saw us across. It was a long, easy ascent, but the ride along the ridge that forms the summit proved bitterly cold. The strong wind that drove the snow along, obliterating the trail under deep drifts, convinced one of with what ease the pass could collect its toll from the caravan rash enough to attempt the crossing in the face of a blizzard.

As we descended we could see stretched out beneath us the Vale of Kashmir. Wular Lake was largely hidden by billowy clouds. At our feet the men pointed out the village of Bandipur, and each showed us the little hamlet in the valley where his house lay. We left the pack-train and took a short cut down the mountainside; it was steep and slippery, but we swung along, grabbing at branches and bushes, jumping from rock to rock, and taking many of the falls that we risked. Once in the valley we had a four-mile walk to the cluster of houses where Rahima and Khalil lived. As we cut through the villages the inmates hurried out to greet Rahima and ask him news of our success. It was his triumphal homecoming, and, though enjoying it to the full, he maintained a stoical and expressionless impressive dignity throughout.

That afternoon the kitchens at Rahima's and Khalil's saw no idle moment. There was no pause in the clatter of pots and pans, and no halt in the roasting and boiling and basting and all the intricacies of preparation of a Kashmir feast. That evening at dinner course succeeded course, each complicated pilaff or roast or stew more delicious than the last. All our stored energy and the physique built by months of mountain-climbing were called upon to enable us to survive the effects of such feasting.

Next morning we were ferried across the lake in dugouts. After seven months we were back in the land of motor transport, but to us it seemed outlandish to make in an hour what had been for so long the distance of a long day's march. That evening our wives met us at Srinagar, and our expedition into central Asia was a closed chapter; a memory of glorious days on the high Himalayas, of long stalks, some successful, some otherwise, of bitter-cold days and snug evenings in Kirghiz yourts; a kaleidoscope of toil and achievement that only experience can purchase.

APPENDIX

A SERAI

BY THEODORE ROOSEVELT

(SUGGESTED BY KERMIT SAYING TO ME WHILE WE SAT IN THE SERAI AT SHAMBA
BAZAAR THAT PERHAPS MARCO POLO HAD BEEN THERE)

The day is gently drawing to a close;
The caravan, slow-plodding through the dusk,
With tinkling bells and creaking leather,
Leaves the rough jungle by the broad brown river
And turns into the cultivated land.
It jogs along by fields, bright green, mud-walled
And fringed with shimmering willows,
Which look to be embroidered on the landscape
Like figures in some ancient tapestry.
At length the dusty column sights a village
Whose rough gray walls are set in lofty poplars
Which seem to stroke the sky with slender fingers.
Down the long street it jingles,
Through the bazaar where ill-wove matting roofs
Add to the gathering gloom;
Where smells of every sort hang in the air,
And bare, brown babies splash in muddy gutters.
At last the dingy old serai is reached.
The tired ponies pass its battered gate,
Then packs are stripped and all is wild confusion;
Shouted commands and loud and shrill abuse,
And stallions neighing, blend in one great babble.
And now the horses fed, the baggage piled,
The fires begin to glow, and round them gather
Dim half-seen figures in the flickering light,
Who squat and eat and puff their gurgling hookahs.
Now in a near-by stall a singer twangs
On some stringed instrument of old design,
And drones an endles plaintive melody.
Out on the near-by roofs the women steal,—
Black silent figures 'gainst the flat gray sky.
So comes the night, and so has come the night
Through dim unreckoned countless generations
To those who travel the old trails of Asia.
In this same way old Marco the Venetian travelled,
And even then the trails were very old.
So Asia does, so she has done since time,
And when our great hotels are piles of stones
And all our railroads briar-grown embankments,
So Asia still will do.

APPENDIX

The following is an itinerary of the expedition from the time we arrived at Srinagar to the day we returned. The mileage is necessarily only approximate, for we had to depend upon information from the natives of the country and check it up roughly with our estimated speed and the number of hours spent in marching. The place names are in general spelled as they sounded when repeated to us, so they are, of course, subject to revision upon the opinion of any hearer.

	MILES		DATE	
Srinagar	12	Gandabal	May	19
	17	Camp (near Gund)	"	20
	12	Camp (near Sonamurg)	"	21
	18	Baltal	"	22
(Zoji Pass)	14	Camp	"	24
	18	Draz	"	25
	22	Shimsa Kharbu	"	26
	16	Karghil	"	27
	22	Mulbekh	"	28
	15	Bod Kharbu	"	29
	15	Lamayuru	"	30
	17	Nurla	June	1
	25	Nimoo	"	2
	12	Leh	"	3
	10	Camp near Pass	"	6
(Khardong Pass)	18	Khardong	"	7
	14	Karsar	"	8
	14	Taghar	"	9
	15	Panamik	"	10
	14	Choong Loong	"	13
	12	Tutyalak	"	14
	13	Camp at foot of Saser Glacier	"	17
(Saser Pass)	10	Brangza Saser	"	18
	16	Remo Glacier	"	19
	24	Murgu	"	20
	20	Kizil Tash	"	21
	23	Daulat Beg Ouldi	"	22

APPENDIX

280

APPENDIX

	MILES		DATE
(Karakoram Pass)....	22	Brangsa........................	June 23
	12	Camp..........................	" 24
	24	Chibra.........................	" 25
(Suget Pass).........	25	Camp..........................	" 26
	6	Suget Karaul...................	" 27
	16	Ulbek (Kara Kash River)........	" 28
	22	Camp at foot of Bostan Valley....	" 29
	20	Ali Nazar Khurgan..............	" 30
(Sanju Pass).........	20	Ayalak........................	July 1
	18	Akas Aghzi.....................	" 3
	12	Kivas..........................	" 4
	16	Sanju Bazar....................	" 5
	24	Kosh Tagh.....................	" 6
	31	Bora..........................	" 7
	18	Karghalik......................	" 8
	35	Posgam........................	" 10
	24	Yarkand.......................	" 11
	26	Tograghi.......................	" 14
	25	Merket........................	" 15
	25	Akadong.......................	" 16
	21	Khandi........................	" 17
	28	Beyond Aksak Maral............	" 18
	27	Maralbashi.....................	" 19
	16	Char Bagh.....................	" 20
	21	Akh Tam......................	" 21
	23	Yakka Kudak...................	" 22
	28	Chillam........................	" 23
	22	Hangoon.......................	" 24
	23	Yanghi Shahr...................	" 25
	4	Aksu..........................	" 26
	27	Jom...........................	" 29
	16	Arbat.........................	" 30
	22	Khurgan.......................	" 31
	18	Camp	Aug. 1
	22	Tango Tash....................	" 2
(Muzart Pass).......	20	Khan Ayalak...................	" 3
	25	Shutta........................	" 6
	25	Agyas.........................	" 7
	30	Moin Tai......................	" 8
	18	Kukteruk......................	" 9
	17	Kooksu........................	" 10
	18	Chungtai	" 11

APPENDIX

MILES		DATE	
16	Chin Bulak.....................	Aug.	12
20	Camp at head of Jilgalong Valley..	"	13
20	Kargaitash.....................	"	14
15	Camp on upper Kooksu..........	"	17
6	Kargaitash Creek...............	"	20
15	Muzdumas Creek...............	"	21
10	Camp..........................	"	23
14	Kensu.........................	"	24
12	Wapiti Camp...................	"	29
8	Camp at junction of Kensu and Kooksu.....................	Sept.	1
18	Camp..........................	"	2
20	Lower Torotai Valley............	"	3
25	Chilukteruk....................	"	4
22	Camp..........................	"	5
16	Moin Tai.......................	"	6
30	Agyas.........................	"	9
8	Camp..........................	"	10
33	Shutta.........................	"	11
25	Khan Ayalak...................	"	12
(Muzart Pass).......20	Tango Tash....................	"	14
18	Khailak.......................	"	15
20	Kizil Bulak....................	"	16
18	Jom...........................	"	17
27	Aksu..........................	"	19
20	Aikul..........................	"	20
40	Chillam........................	"	21
28	Yakka Kudak...................	"	22
30	Toum Shouk....................	"	23
30	Maralbashi....................	"	24
30	Karakuchin....................	"	25
40	Kara Youlgoun.................	"	26
34	Faizabad......................	"	27
45	Kashgar.......................	"	28
16	Tashmalik.....................	Oct.	3
15	Tookoi........................	"	4
20	Beyond Gezkaraul	"	5
25	Bulun Kul.....................	"	6
15	Kichik Kara Kul................	"	7
15	Subashi Nullah.................	"	9
16	Kara Su.......................	"	12
24	Tagharma.....................	"	14

279

APPENDIX

280

INDEX

Afghanistan route, the, 9
Agyas, 123
Aksu, 164, 197; the start for, 82, 94 ff.; departure from, 202
Akyas, journey to, 186; arrival at, 187; return to, 192
Ali-Nazar-Kurgan, 66, 67
Amban, the, of Karghalik, 76 ff.
Andrews, Roy Chapman, expeditions in Asia, 2, 3, 7
Antelope, the Tibetan, description of, 63
Arbat, 199
Arkal, herd of, spotted in the Russian Pamirs, 250
Asboe, Doctor and Mrs., 48
Asia, central, Mongol tribes in, 2
Astore, grave of Lieutenant Davison in, 269
Avalanches, in Baltal, 29, 34, 35
Ayalik, arrival at, 72, 79, 132
Azak-Karaul, Kalmuks in, 122

Bahadur Khan, the, 47, 48
Bai, Tula, 129 ff.; 164, 180
Bakker, Bob, 14
Baltal, avalanches in, 29, 34, 35
Baltistan, 36; Rajah of, 35, 36
Baltit, 265 ff.
Bam-i-Dunya, 252
Bandipur, 273
Barr, 23
Bear, the great brown, 5, 34; sighted by Khalil Loon, 149; shot by Kermit Roosevelt, 150; skinning of, 151
Bey, Ishmael, 104, 113, 198, 199
Bighorn, Rocky Mountain, 38
Birds of prey, 57
Blacker, Major, 24, 25
Bokharan, the, 114
Bombay, landing at, 22, 23
Bombay Natural History Museum, the, 22
Bulun, 219
Bulun Lake, arrival at, 219

Bunji, 268
Burden, Douglas, 25
Burrhel, 53 ff.; capture of, 55
Burroughs, John, 2
Burzil Pass, 269; marmot spotted in the, 271
Butterflies, 29

Camels, 62
Chalt, 259
Cherrie, George K., 6, 11, 13, 17, 23, 28, 45, 49, 52, 56, 66, 67, 69, 82, 83, 94, 170, 182, 183, 184, 185, 186, 193, 195, 199, 204, 212; illness of, 183
Chillum Chauki, 270
Chin Ballak, 127
Chukors, red-legged, in Maralbashi, 91
Cock, black, collected, by Theodore Roosevelt, 186
Cutting, Suydam, 6, 17, 18, 26, 45, 49, 52, 56, 66, 76, 81, 82, 84, 89, 166, 182, 184, 185, 186, 187, 188, 194, 199, 204, 212; photography done by, 183

Daulet Beg Uldi, 62
Davies, Mr. 5
Deer, Siberian roe, 26
Depsang Plain, the, 67; ducks in, 68
Dotai, the, 95, 96
Ducks, in Depsang Plain, 68

Faizabad, 206
Feroze, 25, 27, 82
Ferrets, glimpse of, 147
Fezildin, in charge of dogs, 59, 165
Field, Stanley, 5
Field Museum of Natural History in Chicago, 5, 28
Finches, purple, at the oases, 33; in Maralbashi, 91
Foxes, large red, 138
Foxie, death of, 75

Ganderbal, 27

INDEX

INDEX

INDEX